Reconcilable Differences

Reconcilable Differences

Expanded Edition with Study Guide

Jim Talley
with
Leslie H. Stobbe

THOMAS NELSON PUBLISHERS
NASHVILLE

Published in Nashville, Tennessee, by Thomas Nelson, Inc.

ISBN 0-8407-3196-5

Printed in the United States of America

21 22 QW 07 06 05

C O N T E N T S

P R E F A C E

If you feel this book's topic is too hot to handle without fireproof gloves, join the crowd of people who have sat in my office and were ready to throw darts at me when I used the word *reconciliation*. I'm convinced some of them would have preferred jumping off the Golden Gate Bridge to attending a reconciliation seminar. Yet even when feelings are that strong, there are *reconcilable differences* between estranged marriage partners.

Through many years of counseling the divorced, I have found that attempts at reconciliation are not an all or nothing proposition. The only possible results of these attempts are not simply remarriage or continued hostilities. Many steps (and stops) along the path of reconciliation can reduce the high stress of anger, bitterness, resentment, the "I'll get even with that _____ yet" syndrome.

For the sake of your sanity, you owe it to yourself to reduce your stomach acid build-up when you think of your ex, when you have to call to arrange a weekend with the children, when you have to look for the fifth day in the mailbox for a child support payment that still isn't there. And you can do it without losing self-esteem, respect among your peers, and the support of your children.

Your children deserve your mature attempts to take at least the first steps along the road to reconciliation. You need to do it to reduce the chances of your child's picture appearing on a supermarket bag or on a milk carton. You need to try it so that you won't have to meet on the courthouse steps every time you exchange your children with your ex.

If you happen to have a personal relationship with Jesus Christ, reconciliation takes on a whole new significance. After all, He came not only to reconcile us to Himself but also to reconcile us to others.

For starters, this book is about reconciliation to the friendship level, to the point where you can face your ex and converse in a normal, human way. If that's all you even dare think about, stop here and start reading Chapter One.

This book doesn't stop at the friendship level, though. It takes you all the way to the unthinkable, reconciliation to the point of remarriage. John and Judy and Jim and Bonnie are just two of the couples who have progressed to remarriage after five or more years of divorce. Their experiences prove that even people who have had loveless marriages and hostile divorces can become reconciled to each other. These two couples have built good, solid relationships and have developed true love, and they consider the energy expended in the process to be amply rewarded in their maturing love relationships. (For other personal stories in this book, the names and identifying features have been changed.)

So hear me out. I've seen enough miracles to believe you can experience one too.

This Thing Called "Reconciliation"

The credit manager at the department store was very nice. As he talked with you, he checked off one box after another on the credit application. Then he hit a nerve.

"Married?"

You paused for a split second, halting the automatic response built in through five years of marriage.

"No," you said, but the mental parade wouldn't stop. You remembered the day you looked into that special person's eyes and said, "I love you," for the first time. You were sure you meant those words, but today the slightest thought of your marriage to that person rekindles bitter feelings. Even hearing the word *married* is enough to set you off and get your stomach acid flowing.

Now suppose I mention the word *reconciliation*. How do you respond? Do you panic, tune me out, or become angry? You are perfectly normal if those are your reactions. I see them all the time. Some people I counsel are so angry they think they could cheerfully kill their ex, and when I suggest a workshop on reconciliation, they immediately (and sometimes explosively) reject the idea.

You see, they think reconciliation means remarriage. Yet to be reconciled is not necessarily inviting a former spouse into the house again. At first it may only mean reducing the danger level when children are exchanged for visits.

A California couple, for example, tired of beating each other about the head verbally and physically each time they exchanged their children, now meet on the steps of the city's police station. They find they can be more civil to each other when they are away from the old battlefield of the home. They are not smiling at each other yet, but they have taken the first step toward reconciliation.

Others have a tougher time overcoming the hostility in a broken relationship. For example, after the divorce, Dick remarried and moved three hundred miles away. When he wants to find out about his three sons, he has to use the telephone. He has been doing this for five years now, but he still becomes unsettled every time he calls his children.

"I just know that before the conversation with my sons' mother is over, I am going to get angry—and I hate it," he confesses. "I pay my child support on time, and she still finds ways to get to me."

Yet reconciliation is possible in this situation too. And things would be much smoother for everyone concerned if it were effected. Life is difficult enough without people inflicting needless pain on each other.

The need for reconciliation does not occur only after years of marriage. Reconciliation may be necessary very early in a marriage. In one of my groups, a couple who had been married only three days separated. He filed for divorce. I began working with him so he would at least begin to be civil to her.

Sometimes the first reconciliation has to be to geography; that is, the people involved have to be able to remain in the same room or location for a period of time. In this particular case, as part of therapy, I met the woman at a large social function and said, "Okay, there are a lot of people in there. Let's go in."

"Is he in there?" she asked.

"Yes," I said as I opened the door and pushed her in.

I stood in the hallway, watching the four doors, and sure enough, one of them popped open and he came out just like a jack-in-the-box. I could see I still had a long way to go before I effected reconciliation for them.

I have used the word *reconciliation* several times so far, and I have also touched on the need for it. So what is reconciliation all about? The primary goal of reconciliation, as I will discuss it in this book, is to enable those of you who are angry, bitter, and hostile to be friendly again and bring back harmony, whether you are separated, divorced, or remarried. I will try to do this by helping you better understand yourself and your ex, by developing ways you may cope with potential areas of conflict, and by sharing steps you can take to defuse your anger.

Some Terms You Need to Know

Let me explain certain words I will use to describe stages that people go through as they relate to each other.

1. Friendship

I define *friendship* as "a deep and enduring affection built on mutual respect and esteem." It is genderless, which means you do the same things with either sex. It is nonexclusive, which indicates you may have many friends of both sexes. The support provided by a strong circle of friends makes you a better candidate for the next level of a relationship.

Unfortunately, many people say they do not want friends because that level of commitment is too low. They want a genuine relationship. Yet none of us is ready to handle the demands of a relationship until we have established the fact that we can operate at the friendship level with both males and females.

11

2. Relationship

When friends develop an intimate reliance upon each other, they have entered into a *relationship*. There are many kinds of relationships, but the relationship I refer to here is gender oriented—focused on the opposite sex—and mutually exclusive. That is, you can have only one at a time.

Many a seventeen-year-old, and a surprising number of older singles, attempt to cycle through three or four relationships at a time. Determined to find the best possible combination through an A, B, or C process of evaluation, these people can get into deep trouble.

How do you know when you have moved from friendship to a relationship? The clearest indicator is when you start doing things with the opposite sex you would not do comfortably with someone of the same sex. Once that happens, you have crossed the line from being a friend to entering into a relationship. All the rules change at that point, and you'd better know when that happens.

3. Marriage

I use the term *marriage* to describe "the union of two people in an emotional, moral, and legal convenantal agreement." Be aware of the dynamics of all three facets of marriage: emotional, moral, *and* legal. This will be especially important when we talk about separation, divorce, and remarriage, since emotional and moral aspects cannot be treated as easily as the legal aspect.

4. Divorce

A *divorce* represents "the severing of the marital covenant by a legal decree and the sundering of the relationship." The legal aspect is eventually finalized when the decree is issued, but recognizing such a finality of the moral and emotional parts is much less easy to accomplish.

To describe what a divorce does to the emotional part of marriage, I used the word *sundering*. There is a ragged, rough tearing apart of a relationship. That is why it is so difficult to put back together again.

People make their biggest mistake when they feel they can deal with the moral and emotional parts simply by walking out and saying they are not in love anymore. Or they will walk out on a Friday night and feel free—free to date and do what they want, although they have not dealt with the legal aspects of marriage. Sooner or later their miscalculation catches up with them.

5. Reconciliation

In *reconciliation* people begin to deal with the moral and emotional parts, for the goal is to be friendly again and to bring back harmony. (Notice that the word *marriage* does not enter into the discussion here.)

A quick look at the British legal system may help. A conciliator works for the divorce court as a sort of family counselor. This person's goal is to conciliate the differences between the parties in the divorce and to reduce the hostility level so they can be friends again.

I say that reconciliation has been accomplished when both of you can carry on normal human communication. This is a goal to achieve at whatever your legal, moral, or emotional level. Your stomach does not knot up, your blood pressure does not rise anymore, and your voice does not rise in verbal communication. You are able to communicate with each other as you would with any person in your circle of acquaintances.

A Goal Worth Tackling

Is that a goal worth tackling? Is it worth spending a few hours reading a book and many more in special effort? I think it is, and many people I have counseled agree that it is.

John and Judy were nineteen years old when they first met. They were in the air force at the time. John drove a truck, and Judy was a medic.

"Our barracks were not far apart, and one day I saw her walking toward her barracks. I decided I wanted to get to know her," recalls John.

They met at poolside.

"I swim like a rock, so we did a lot of sunbathing," he says. "I thought she was the most beautiful thing I had ever seen."

"And I thought he was so tall and good looking! I am five nine and love to wear high heels, so I get to be nearly six feet tall. And it was great to be able to look up to someone," says Judy.

They were married in the chapel at the base one year after first meeting. Greg came along quickly to cement the relationship as a family, and Dean was born four years later.

Once he got out of the service, John became a long-distance truck driver.

"I used to worry about his safety on his long trips. He would drive up to three days without sleeping. But I really didn't worry about anything else," Judy says.

John, on the other hand, found that there were a lot of eligible relationships on the road.

"I was not really serious about keeping our marriage together. I didn't really recognize the value of marriage, so I felt that the grass was always greener outside of my marriage," John says.

A vague dissatisfaction became a conviction that he should opt out of marriage.

"I can't really tell you why that dissatisfaction grew. Maybe it was because Judy began gaining weight after Greg was born, but I can't really put my finger on it," he recalls.

Judy never lost her love for John. As far as she was concerned, he was the best thing that had happened to her. Since she had grown up on a farm and developed self-sufficiency, she did not really mind coping with having her own job, doing all the work at home, and raising two boys while John was on the road.

"When he came home, he had a big home-cooked meal and poured out everything that had happened, all the frustrations and hassles. Then about eight-and-one-half years into our marriage I began to notice that he was not doing the sharing anymore. He came home angry, ate, and went to bed. And he would soon be off and on the road again," she reports.

One day John announced that he was leaving and wanted a divorce.

"I didn't do it nicely. I just blurted it out," he says.

Judy was stunned and angry. She was unable to really recognize why John wanted out of the marriage.

"He insisted that if I did not file for divorce, he would. We lived in Florida at the time, so we got our divorce in twenty-one days," Judy says.

Judy was the first to recognize her need for a personal faith in Jesus Christ. After that, "He wanted to come back again, so I let him live with me for a year. But I felt more and more guilty about it, so I asked him to leave," Judy says. They were divorced for six years, although they actually lived together off and on for the first three-and-a-half years.

Two years after that, John had a motorcycle accident in which he was injured, although he did not need hospitalization.

"I finally realized how bankrupt I really was. Then I remembered the little booklet, 'The Four Spiritual Laws,' that Judy had given me when she asked me to leave. I never kept anything, but for some reason I had kept this booklet. I found it and read it, praying the prayer of commitment," he says.

The next Sunday morning Judy could not believe her eyes when she saw John walk the aisle to the front of the church as a public confirmation of his commitment to Jesus Christ.

"I thought immediately that everything would be all right now, that we could get back together again. But his coming to faith in Christ didn't instantly solve everything," she says.

Gradually John realized that God was asking him to return to the relationship with Judy that he had abandoned.

"Through Scripture and as I thought about it, the Lord impressed me that we needed to be together again," he says.

The start was dinner at Judy's house, and the conclusion was a quick ceremony of remarriage before a justice of the peace in Reno in 1979.

How are they doing six years later?

"There were times after we remarried I wondered what I had done. I wasn't really that committed to him, but John's commitment to me was so deep. I could see how committed he was in the way he was determined to work out our problems—and that increased my commitment to him," Judy reports.

John says, "Jesus committed Himself to me when He died on the cross for me. Out of that commitment flows my commitment to His will for my life, and His will clearly is that I be married to Judy. That then becomes the basis of my commitment to Judy."

What John says points to a vital step in reconciliation. The apostle Paul described the process as follows, "Now all these things are from God, who reconciled us to Himself through Christ, and gave us the ministry of reconciliation, namely, that God was in Christ reconciling the world to Himself, not counting their trespasses against them, and He has committed to us the word of reconciliation" (2 Cor.

5:18–19). Once John had become reconciled to God through personal faith in Jesus and His death on the cross for us, he realized that he needed to be reconciled to Judy. Personal peace with God meant he could shift his efforts to achieving peace with his ex-wife.

That doesn't mean that absolute peace descended on his relationship with Judy. It took a year of effort for true reconciliation to take place and then daily effort to maintain the new relationship.

Even the great apostle Paul experienced a damaging rupture in a relationship at a time when he was ecstatic over the results of his first missionary trip. He and Barnabas enjoyed a marvelous reception as they reported on what God had done. But the time came for a second tour of the newly formed churches, and Paul sat down with Barnabas to discuss the travel arrangements.

"Paul, I think we ought to take John Mark along again as an intern. I know he abandoned us midway through the first trip, but I think he has learned his lesson. He will not be a quitter again," said Barnabas.

"Can't stand quitters. Never have and never will. He's not going along. We can do without him," Paul seems to have responded hotly. The historian Luke reported, "And there arose such a sharp disagreement that they separated from one another" (Acts 15:39).

Barnabas left with John Mark on his own tour, and Paul set out with Silas. Years went by. In his last letter, written while he was in prison in Rome, Paul charged Timothy, "Pick up Mark and bring him with you, for he is useful to me for service" (2 Tim. 4:11). Clearly, there had been a reconciliation!

Now just suppose you were to seriously consider reconciliation as a possible step to relaxing tensions and personal stress. What are some of the reasons you should make the effort? Could the reason for the sundering of your marriage relationship be rooted in some basic differences between the sexes? What if you make the move and are rejected? Should you give up or remain in a conciliatory mode? What are the steps you can take to begin anew on a friendship basis? What happens if you suddenly discover you are in love again? (Stranger things have happened!) Can two angry, bitter, hostile, and fed-up-with-it-all former marriage partners actually remarry and make a success of it? Stay with me as we explore the answers to these and other questions I am asked as I counsel separated and divorced persons.

Why Make
the Effort?

Have you ever attended an auction where people bid on a mystery box, hoping that something of value would be in it? Maybe you refused to join the bidding because you would rather spend your money on an item you had time to check out.

Or you may have had an experience similar to that of our friends. They were part of a group that had a white elephant gift exchange each Christmas. As people arrived, they placed their packages on a pile in the center of the living room floor. While refreshments were served, each person pulled a number from a hat. Later they gathered in a circle around the pile. The person with number one selected a gift and opened it. The guest with number two could choose between any gift in the pile or the one already opened. In sequence, each guest could choose between the unknown quality in the gifts on the floor or the already visible quality of the opened gifts.

One year our friends decided to take a large, well-wrapped package instead of any of the already opened gifts. To their dismay, they unwrapped a heavy wooden gate. Their willingness to risk the unknown got them a true white elephant, a gate for which they had no use on their property.

Maybe some of you are facing a similar choice. You can

choose to re-establish friendship with the spouse from whom you are separated or divorced, or you can go the white elephant route and initiate a totally new relationship with someone you have met only in social or work situations. The risk of landing a white elephant is high, yet each year more than one million people take that risk.

Remember John and Judy? Though they had been divorced for six years, both admit they never met anyone with the qualities they had appreciated in each other. Even his fascination with motorcycle racing did not provide the satisfactions John had experienced in marriage.

Judy reports, "I was open to other relationships. When I did look, the people I looked at were far less attractive than John."

Let's consider some of the reasons why re-establishing friendship with a former mate is more attractive than continuing to open boxes of unknown value in terms of a relationship. When you stop to think about it, why not build a relationship with the person with whom you have had the most experience?

1. Each Marriage Relationship Represents a Valuable Heritage.

I can hear you say, "You certainly don't know my ex." That may be true, but my counseling of many divorced singles has shown me the significance of commonly shared activities as bonding agents, even though many of the experiences were negative. The bond has been broken, but the heritage of experiences remains.

The memories started building when you began dating. You can name the place you met, the restaurants you frequented, the football or baseball games you attended together. Maybe you enjoyed music, and concerts became rich times of sharing. Visits to friends and relatives at Thanksgiving or Christmas were woven into the fabric of your growing marriage.

Then the children came, and you spent nights awake with a child who had a fever or colic. You may remember school days, visits with the children's teachers, trips to the zoo, picnics in nearby parks, games on Saturday afternoons, and expeditions to a favorite ice cream parlor. Your storehouse of memories differs radically from mine, but the heritage is there and it represents a level of shared experiences you have had with no one else.

Suppose you were to drop your guard and forget your anger for a few minutes. Wouldn't you have a lot to talk about with your ex? You might even remember some of the lighter moments, the times you laughed together as you did ridiculous things or pulled practical jokes on each other.

Remember, that heritage is a reservoir of experiences you can draw on when you begin to reconcile and to rebuild friendship with your ex and the family. You may want to take time right now to write out a list of ten enjoyable experiences you have had together. Use this list to try to recapture some of the good moments you spent together. This may be hard, but it is vital to your process of recovery. What about the honeymoon or special trips you made together? Or family gatherings or special gifts? Don't forget to focus on the fun times.

That is what John and Judy found when, after six years of divorce, John returned for dinner. Sure, he and Judy were nervous, but the nine years they had lived together as husband and wife had not vanished in a sea of total forgetfulness.

Recently an uncle asked the oldest son what he thought of his father and mother remarrying. "It's a really good thing," he said, reflecting on the six years his parents had been together after six years of divorce. Another layer of experiences, another collection of heritage pieces, had been added, and they were good.

2. *Friendship Removes the Stress of Negative Emotions.*

Let's face it. No one really wants a divorce. Most spouses have to be pushed hard before they will take action. Judy was like that.

"I didn't want the divorce. John insisted on it. He told me that if I didn't divorce him, he would divorce me. After we were divorced I was very angry at him. I hated what he had done to me," she says.

"Sorry, but that's not me," you may be saying. "It was good riddance of the bum, and I couldn't get rid of him fast enough for what he had done to me."

If these are your feelings, you are still stoking the fires of anger and hatred. You may just love to make him squirm when he comes to pick up the children. Yet what are the real benefits of keeping such negative emotions bubbling? How do they affect your blood pressure? What do they do to your sleep? In what ways do they affect your relationship with your children? Children are more sensitive to such feelings than you might realize.

The Bible has a lot to say about what all this negativity can do to you: "Cease from anger, and forsake wrath; Fret not yourself, it leads only to evildoing" (Ps. 37:8); "Do not be eager in your heart to be angry/For anger resides in the bosom of fools" (Eccl. 7:9); and "The one who says he is in the light and yet hates his brother is in the darkness" (1 John 2:9). A Christian life filled with these emotions will not be able to develop as God intends it to develop and the Christian will not be able to live for God and His glory.

We are told that the God of hope will fill us "with all joy

and peace in believing, that [we] may abound in hope" (Rom. 15:13). Don't allow your negative emotions to crowd out all the positive emotions that we as Christians are to have. Remember, "a joyful heart makes a cheerful face" (Prov. 15:13) and "a joyful heart is good medicine" (Prov. 17:22).

Someday take a piece of paper and draw a line down the middle. At the top on the left side write "Negative Emotions" and on the right put "Positive Emotions." List the benefits of these negative emotions in your life and your children's lives, and then list the benefits of positive emotions such as love, joy, and thanksgiving. Think of specific applications of both negative and positive emotions.

Even though you may never get beyond a normal friendship level with your former spouse, you need the emotional stability that positive emotions give you. You need the support of your former spouse in dealing with your children who learn quickly that they can play one against the other when Mom and Dad don't agree.

My folks went through a separation when I was twelve years old. When I was in the eighth grade, my class was to go on a field trip, and I needed some money. I went to my mother and said, "I need some money." She gave me ten dollars. Since my parents were not communicating, I went to Dad, told him about the field trip, and got another ten dollars. In those days that was a lot of money to take along on a Catalina Island weekend. I had learned how to take advantage of their separation—even if I was dishonest.

Resentment and anger only tear us apart and set us up for emotionally damaging retaliation. Recently a young girl moved in with her father. To get back at her mother, she asked for all her baby things. Her mother refused because she felt the girl wasn't responsible enough yet to take care of them. The father hired an attorney and filed suit against the mother to get the baby things. Imagine the emotional stress of facing each other in court.

3. *Children Encourage Reconciliation.*

Children have a powerful desire for family unity. They will go to any lengths to prevent divorce from happening. If they have been unable to stop it, they will embark on the wildest schemes to get their parents together. Some of the funniest movies depict children's efforts to effect reconciliation.

This desire for two parents is the cause for much of the distress when two families unite. Children will take anyone who will make their family seem whole again. The kids will try to turn anyone the mother dates into a father image.

"Are you going to be my daddy?" is the first question men will hear when they date a single mother. Children are trying to build a heritage again as rapidly as they can, and they inevitably overlook anything that the man does wrong. They pay little attention to character deficiencies or areas of conflict.

But when the new marriage occurs, everything seems to come unraveled. Suddenly, "I don't like him" or "I don't like the way he..." become common refrains. When the other asks, "Why didn't you say anything when we were going together?" the children say, "We wanted to be a family."

Frankly, I don't think adults understand how intense and how deeply ingrained that drive to be a whole family is in children. Nor do we recognize how much of a positive force it is in reconciliation.

4. *Reconciliation Makes Economic Sense.*

Even though two cannot live cheaper than one, the dynamic changes that occur after a separation force both partners to suffer economically. The effect is intensified when they have children.

"Don't I know it," you may be saying. "I'm one of the new poor discussed in the newspapers. Living on welfare with four preschoolers is the most debasing thing I've experienced."

Wives are not the only ones to have joined the ranks of those living below the poverty level. Many husbands go through such emotional alienation that they lose their jobs and find it difficult to get another one. Or even if the husband keeps his job, he will have the cost of child support and perhaps alimony added to the cost of maintaining a second residence. As a result, he will have little or no discretionary income. Should he marry another single parent, he will have to provide for two families, and that is not an easy task to accomplish for most people.

Small wonder that during the recession of 1981–1983 the number of remarriages declined significantly. The jobs were simply not there to support two families, and the man who may have walked out in 1979 suddenly thought twice. Also many could not afford the attorney fees required to finalize a divorce.

We don't like to think about the really tough financial situations people can get themselves into as a result of a marital breakup. After a friend of mine filed for divorce, he got into a real battle over a property settlement, and he finally sold his house. At that point he decided to reconcile with his wife, and he moved into an apartment with her.

Sometime later I asked them where they were living.

They said, "Well, we are still living in an apartment. Since we sold all the furniture after we sold the house, we are starting all over again."

Unfortunately, this scenario is repeated over and over again. When you looked ahead toward the divorce, you thought you would simply split the property and all the other assets. That is seldom how it works. In reality you add up all the assets and divide that by four. When the divorce is final, she gets one fourth, he gets another fourth, and the two attorneys split the rest. Stabilizing your finances by reconciling before a divorce means you won't get into this problem and end up paying your money to someone else.

But let's say you go ahead and get the divorce. What if you are exemplary and make every support payment on time? What hope is there of getting an adjustment or of doing something special for one or more of the children? The only hope you have is that you are able to effect a reconciliation. It is amazing how an improving emotional climate can result in reduced financial demands. If a person is willing to listen and gain an understanding of the other person's needs, that creates the kind of good will that makes breakthroughs possible.

5. Most Divorced Persons Recycle to a Similar Mate.

I had some really close friends who got married. Dave is not a dynamic person; he is a committed, plodding, loyal, and faithful guy. He never likes to make decisions, nor does he like conflict. The fact is, Dave is not a leader.

Joan finally got her fill of Dave and his inability and unwillingness to make decisions. He was much too passive for her. So she divorced him and married another guy. I have met her new husband, and I think he is more indecisive than Dave. I think she even had to propose to him! Guess how long that marriage is going to last.

Counselors who work with families broken up as a result of alcoholism report that the wife of an alcoholic husband typically remarries an alcoholic. One clinic was trying to help a woman who had had seven husbands, all alcoholics. She was incredibly resistant to making any changes that would prevent her marrying an eighth alcoholic.

6. Reconciliation Paves the Way for Stability.

The saddest comments I have ever heard are from couples who are married for the second time. When I ask them, "Well, how's it going?" they respond, "The marriage is going really good. We are working hard at it. We are building a life together. It's really going great." But then they add, "You know, if I had just put half as much energy into reconciling, I could have saved my first marriage."

If you can reconcile early enough, you can help each other stabilize emotionally, and you won't have to endure years of exhausting emotional turmoil. Stability in this area will improve all areas of your life and contribute to your total well-being.

7. God Expects You to Be Reconciled.

I really don't know anything about your personal views, but surveys of attitudes show that 60 per cent of us think that the rule of thumb for actions is, "If it feels good, do it." Whether we are part of the religious left or the religious right doesn't matter much. The majority of us have simply set aside guidelines for life other than our feelings, our own logic.

We have applied that philosophy to our marriage relationships as well. As a result, several million people who call themselves born-again Christians have experienced divorce. It is my experience that they have as much anger, as much bitterness, and as much emotional trauma as non-Christians. And they find it just as hard to accept any authority other than themselves.

Yet we really ought to listen to what the Bible says about the way we live. After all, we accepted what it told us about Jesus' death on the cross for us—about His willingness to forgive our sins and to give us eternal life. If we accept that information as authoritative, why don't we accept what the Bible has to say about marriage and about reconciliation?

In the book of Ephesians the apostle Paul described the reason for the animosity between Jews and non-Jews in the time before Jesus' coming. The non-Jews had been excluded from the blessings of God's covenant with Israel, and in that condition the non-Jews were "separate from Christ, excluded from the commonwealth of Israel, and strangers to the covenants of promise, having no hope and without God in the world" (Eph. 2:12).

I could compare their plight to the husband banished from his house by a wife filing for divorce. There just doesn't seem to be any hope of reversing the situation. Even a mediator probably would be ineffective. Then one day everything changes, and there is reason to have hope.

But now in Christ Jesus you who formerly were far off have been brought near by the blood of Christ. For He Himself is our peace, who made both groups into one, and broke down the barrier of the dividing wall, by abolishing in His flesh the enmity...that in Himself He might make the two into one new man, thus establishing peace, and might reconcile them both in one body to God through the cross, by it having put to death the enmity (Eph. 2:13-16).

"Hold it," you may be saying. "That passage clearly speaks to the enmity between the races, between me as sinner and a righteous God. I accept that He has removed that animosity and replaced it by love. You cannot apply that to my marital situation."

Let me ask you to withhold final judgment while we examine the next verses. "And He came and preached peace to you who were far away, and peace to those who were near;...So then you are no longer strangers and aliens, but you are fellow citizens with the saints, and are of God's household" (Eph. 2:17, 19).

If Jesus "preached peace" to those who are far away, wouldn't He also suggest a return to peace in your relationship to your former husband or wife? I seriously doubt Jesus changes His message very much as He looks over your broken relationship.

Of course, you may say, "That is all fine and good, but simple pronouncements of peace or tranquillity are not going to change anything between us. You don't know how deep the crack is in our relationship."

Okay, let's accept as a premise that your relationship has a deep crack. Where is the most likely place for that crack to be reduced? Paul again provides the answer: "For through Him we both have our access in one Spirit to the Father" (Eph. 2:18). What would you expect to happen between you if you both this moment appeared before God, with the Holy Spirit holding hands with each of you, as it were? Wouldn't you be forced to reconciliation in the presence of the King of peace?

That is in effect what happens every day when two believers pray. You meet in the Spirit in the presence of God, the Father, and worship and adore Him; ultimately you place before Him your petitions. And in your mind and soul you hear Jesus repeat the words He told His disciples: "If therefore you are presenting your offering at the altar, and there remember that your brother [or sister] has something against you, leave your offering there before the altar, and go on your way; first be reconciled to your brother, and then come and present your offering" (Matt. 5:23–24). These words also apply to your ex.

Like a distant roll of thunder, you might also hear Jesus say, "If you forgive men for their transgressions, your heavenly Father will also forgive you. But if you do not forgive men, then your Father will not forgive your transgressions" (Matt. 6:14–15). Jesus did not build any exceptions into that statement. More than likely, you and I would have, because we do not want to admit to our own roles in the alienation. Yet we cannot get away from the black and white of those statements, the either-or-ness of Jesus. He really meant for us to forgive and to be reconciled. If we admit to the authority of Jesus, our course of action is clear: We are to be reconciled.

A rather pointed commentary on this was given by the apostle Paul, "And be kind to one another, tender-hearted, forgiving each other, just as God in Christ also has forgiven you" (Eph. 4:32).

The rewards of reconciliation are enormous. Some we have mentioned, and others we will discuss later. Before we can get into that, however, we need to look at marriage as we are experiencing it today.

What's in a Marriage Anyway?

If marriages are made in heaven, whatever is happening to them on earth? The National Center for Health statistics tell us that in 1981 the average marriage lasted seven years, and remarriage occurred within three years.

Suppose you are married at twenty. Your marriage today will last, on the average, seven years (though some may last sixty years). Should your marriage then break up, you will probably remarry within three years. Now you are thirty, and by thirty-seven you will probably have experienced your second divorce. By the time you are forty you will likely tie the knot for the third time.

Second marriages normally do not last as long as the first, and the third is even shorter than the second. I have counseled people who have been married four or five times and are not yet forty years old.

Some marriages never really get off the ground. I have a friend who married one day and separated from his wife the next. For two years they were never seen together in the same room, but once we got them that close together physically, the process of reconciliation began. Ten months of rebuilding the relationship resulted in their remarrying, but for a long time I simply did not think it would happen.

What had happened? They had made it through the first stage in marriage, the romantic, floating-on-cloud-nine stage. For most people the first twenty-four to forty-eight hours after the wedding ceremony take care of that feeling. When reality sets in, people either let their commitment carry them through or they give up and quit, as this couple did.

For Jim and Bonnie, the commitment made during their December marriage held for fourteen years despite the disenchantment of the first days after the wedding.

"I was really disillusioned the first week after the wedding. I felt that I had probably made a mistake, and I wished I could get out of it," confesses Jim.

Jim and Bonnie had known each other eight months. They commuted between Pomona and Merced, California, on weekends, since he taught in Merced and she was completing her education degree at Pomona. He was unmarried. She had lost her first husband to cancer and was caring for a four-year-old son.

"I was the proverbial 'knight in shining armor' riding to the rescue of a lady in distress. I knew after the wedding that I did not love her, and frankly, I did not respect her. I felt she did not have any guts," says Jim.

Should a couple make it through the disenchantment stage, they begin the process of maturing in marriage. If they have established a basic level of communication, they can work out disagreements and strengthen common interests. If that fails to happen, disintegration sets in.

Jim and Bonnie had not started communicating before the wedding, except on a superficial level involving the trivial affairs of everyday life. The fact that they were married did nothing to improve communication, and their marriage even seemed to suppress it.

"I hated conflict and desperately tried to keep from getting into arguments," remembers Bonnie.

Her behavior only increased Jim's contempt for her because she never stood up to him. Since lack of respect is an obvious hindrance to communication, Jim and Bonnie never did get beyond trivialities, and they both experienced tremendous frustration and tension.

"My stomach was in knots at home all the time," reveals Bonnie.

Couples who develop communication tend to have a useful set of questions: "How do you see it?"; "What can we do to work it out?"; "I'm willing to hang on and see it through. What about you?" Such couples are willing to ask these questions and to honestly consider the responses.

When each individual in a marriage begins to put the other's happiness first and they both begin to learn about constructive confrontation, they enter the third stage of marriage. They begin to establish patterns of accommodation to each other's needs and wishes; they may learn when *not* to bring up issues that arouse anger; and they discover what topics need to be discussed in a restaurant when they are on neutral turf. When a couple achieves these things, they are on their way to a happy married life. If they do not achieve these things, their marriage is headed for trouble.

Remember the First Time?

Figure 3.1 charts the various stages from the time you become acquainted with someone of the opposite sex to the time you get involved with each other sexually, which should happen only in marriage.

What happens in this process? Basically, you move from acquaintanceship to sexual activity during a romantic glow that prevents your becoming friends. Once the romantic glow is off because of the reality of life together, you do not have an adequate relationship basis to work things out. You literally do not know each other, as was the case with Jim and Bonnie.

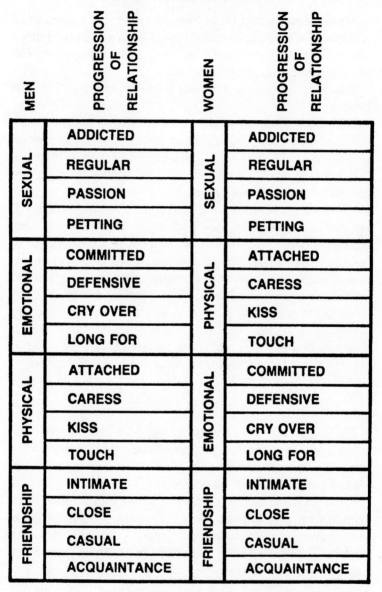

MEN	PROGRESSION OF RELATIONSHIP	WOMEN	PROGRESSION OF RELATIONSHIP
SEXUAL	ADDICTED	**SEXUAL**	ADDICTED
	REGULAR		REGULAR
	PASSION		PASSION
	PETTING		PETTING
EMOTIONAL	COMMITTED	**PHYSICAL**	ATTACHED
	DEFENSIVE		CARESS
	CRY OVER		KISS
	LONG FOR		TOUCH
PHYSICAL	ATTACHED	**EMOTIONAL**	COMMITTED
	CARESS		DEFENSIVE
	KISS		CRY OVER
	TOUCH		LONG FOR
FRIENDSHIP	INTIMATE	**FRIENDSHIP**	INTIMATE
	CLOSE		CLOSE
	CASUAL		CASUAL
	ACQUAINTANCE		ACQUAINTANCE

Fig. 3.1. Interpersonal Relationship Development

34

This is particularly true when two people get married after knowing each other for only a short time. In Figure 3.2 the husband has made no emotional commitment, not to his wife and probably not to their marriage. The wife has a husband and a ring on her finger, but she does not have his heart. In effect they have entered into a live-in relationship in which the bulk of their lives is committed elsewhere. When someone else attractive appears, one of them is likely to break this live-in marital relationship in order to move in with the new arrival on the scene. This happened in Jim's case.

At the other extreme are the two people who once were in love but have not seen each other for many years. They meet again, and they try to pick up where they left off in the relationship. They get married, not having taken the time to rebuild the relationship. Unless they embark on building a marriage relationship based on friendship, they will also run a high risk of going the divorce route.

Developing an Ideal Relationship

Take a look at the number of hours needed for the development of an ideal relationship (see Fig. 3.3). Based on my findings after years of counseling I recommend that you spend approximately 90 hours together in the first four months. Use that time to get to know each other. These numbers are verified by hundreds of couples who have followed these time guidelines. My book *Too Close, Too Soon* will give a complete view of these concepts.

Typically, the man likes to move quickly to the physical level. At this point he normally is not yet emotionally involved. The woman, however, gets involved emotionally much more quickly and usually considers the advance to kissing and caressing an indication of commitment on the man's part.

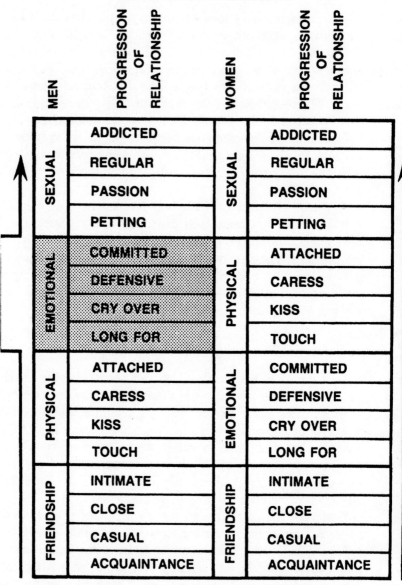

Fig. 3.2. Interpersonal Relationship Development

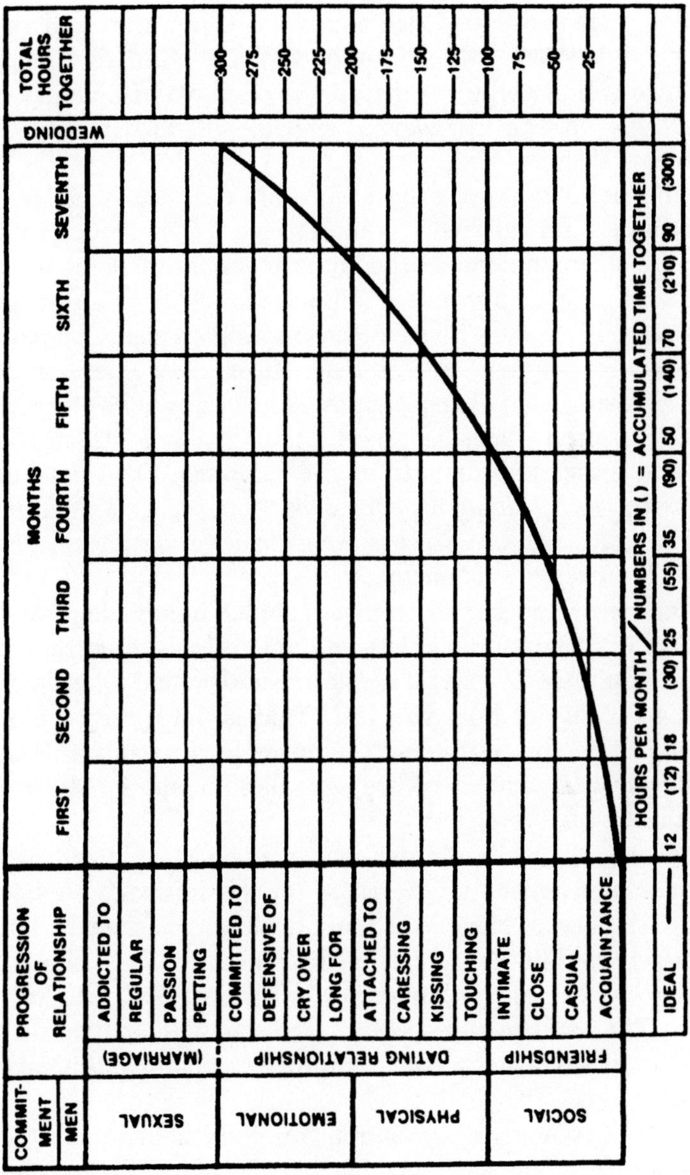

Fig. 3.3. The Talley-Graph Interpersonal Relationship Development Model

Some women experience a broken relationship and become so depressed they cannot function normally. Such women wonder why the man never cried over it. He never even winked—he just waved, smiled, and then turned to someone else.

The fact is that her expectations are different; therefore, the results are different. Look at Figure 3.4. Notice that when the woman crosses the line from an intimate relationship, she moves a whole quadrant. To get from social to physical, she moves through the emotional level. Compare that to the man, who doesn't reach the emotional level until the third quadrant. Thus, as soon as he begins to be physical with her, she assumes he is as emotionally committed as she is. She is therefore open to physical contact. She thinks to herself: *If he is holding my hand and kissing me good night, he must really love me. Because I am involved emotionally, he must be involved emotionally.*

Ladies, he kisses many things: people's hands, dogs, and his car. In his mind there is really not a whole lot of difference. You must be careful not to misunderstand what he is doing because of how you feel. That is not a measure of what is going on in his life. The normal man wants at least some physical contact before he makes an emotional commitment.

You see, the woman progresses in a relationship and sees sexual involvement or marriage on the horizon. So one night she says, "Have you thought about marriage?" His eyes get real big, he catches his breath and says, "I think I need to go. I'll call you tomorrow or the next day." And he is gone. The next time she sees him, he is out with another person, and she crashes to the bottom emotionally and breaks apart.

At the beginning of a relationship both the man and the woman are happy just being together. They are usually open

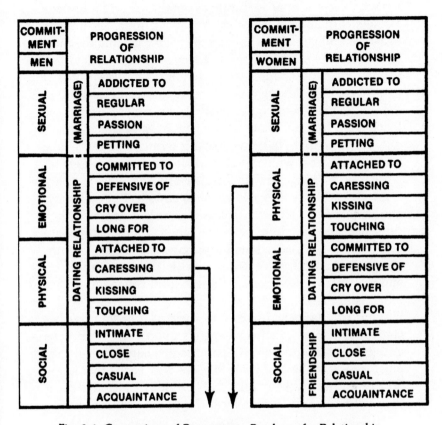

Fig. 3.4. Comparison of Responses to Breakup of a Relationship
for Men and Women if Different Progressions Are Followed

In this example, the relationship had progresssed to the physical level
where the couple were always hanging onto (caressing) one another. For
the man, the return to the level of close friendship was less of a change
than for the woman, who had already made an emotional commitment to
the relationship.

in their acceptance of each other's comments and questions as they learn about each other. Yet as the hours accumulate in a developing relationship and the couple get into the third level, their responses begin to change. I have watched this happen in many couples—even among eighty-year-olds. I refer to it as the "thought response to counsel or authority."

Motives start being questioned: "Why are you asking me that?" or "What do you mean we cannot go out tonight? It's only the third night in a row. What is wrong with that?" She offers advice on what he should do about a problem at work, and he suggests that she alter certain elements of her lifestyle. Suddenly they rebel against any show of authority, and they resent specific inquiries about their actions. They deny any accountability to each other. Their relationship continues to progress, but the progression is not smooth. They have difficulty discussing what is happening to them, and even a friend who offers some helpful comments comes under fire.

What has happened is that as their relationship has become more involved, their demands upon each other have changed. For their relationship to become harmonious, they must recognize this and come to terms with each other in the area of authority. They may suffer serious consequences if they fail to do this, especially if they choose to marry.

Maintaining Harmony

If a couple has not spent the quality time together to establish a harmonious relationship, they move into marriage unprepared for the adjustment in the close confines of an apartment or a home. The wife may walk out and go home to mother for a day or a week; the husband may spend evenings in a bar. Church-related people retreat into church activities.

"I was a Christian, so I buried myself in work at the church. Jim resented this and complained about it, but I got more satisfaction there than being with Jim," says Bonnie.

Today a large majority of couples with this kind of stress decide they really were not meant for each other and get a divorce. All is not lost, however. Friendship can be developed within marriage if both partners are willing to start at the beginning. They have to learn to walk before they can run and that takes time and concentrated effort. For Jim and Bonnie this actually happened four years after they were divorced, when they agreed to friendship instruction. Feelings they had never imagined possible emerged and grew, so they were then willing to enter and complete the friendship phase.

During the next step, Christian counseling can be most helpful. The time Jim and Bonnie spent with me in relationship instruction proved pivotal in keeping them within the limits of harmony needed for reconciliation. (I will explain what is involved in friendship instruction and in relationship instruction in a later chapter.)

Even normal marriages experience periods of stress or disharmony. Figure 3.5 depicts the basic boundaries within which a marriage must remain to maintain harmony. The thick dark line in the middle is called the "line of reconciliation." The outer limits are called the "limits of harmony." Beyond those limits is "disharmony."

A man and a woman get married. In their life together they move back and forth along the center line, the line of reconciliation. As disagreements arise, they deal with them, sometimes quickly but sometimes slowly over several days or weeks. They literally pull apart, then resolve the argument, and get back together again (see Fig. 3.6).

When a couple lock into a friendship, a relationship, or a marriage, their lives are held together by an invisible rubber

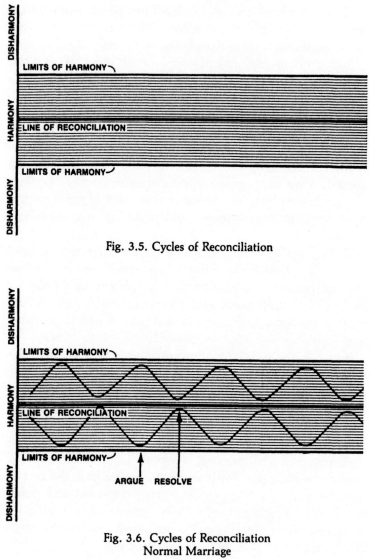

Fig. 3.5. Cycles of Reconciliation

Fig. 3.6. Cycles of Reconciliation
Normal Marriage

band called "homeostasis." The further they pull away from the line of reconciliation, the stronger the force that pulls them back. This holds true even after a separation or a divorce. When the couple go beyond the outer limits of harmony into violent disharmony, homeostasis will eventually draw them to reconciliation.

God created this homeostasis when He brought Eve to life as Adam's life partner: "For this cause a man shall leave his father and his mother, and shall cleave to his wife; and they shall become one flesh" (Gen. 2:24). Even today the mystery continues. When a man and a woman genuinely committed to each other in love and marriage come together in sexual intercourse, that unique guilt-free bonding occurs and they become "one flesh." This is not possible outside of marriage.

The couples that stay within the limits of harmony are not without problems. They simply have developed some skills in conflict resolution. Now that Jim and Bonnie have been remarried two years they have gained experience in this.

"Just because you get married again doesn't mean that everything is peaches and cream. Problems still come, but Bonnie and I have learned how to resolve them. We don't let the sun go down on our disagreements," says Jim.

Alienation—The Stiff Penalty for Disrupted Harmony

People who do not learn how to handle conflict in marriage blast off into the outer limits of disharmony and head straight for divorce. They are angry, bitter, pugnacious, and often determined to hurt their marriage partners. This pattern is illustrated in Figure 3.7.

When this happens, a marriage is sundered in such a way that rough, jagged edges of hurt, anger, and bitterness are left. Many times the two people try to put as much distance between each other as they can. They find it too painful to

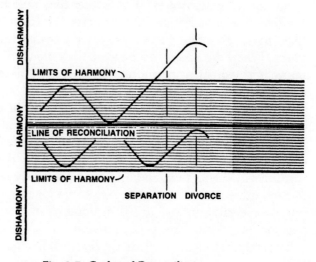

Fig. 3.7. Cycles of Reconciliation
Separation

even see their ex shopping in a store, much less dating someone else.

Because of this sense of belonging together, of being "one flesh," the trauma of divorce creates such a strong emotional upheaval that one or both experience alienation. The alienated person is not merely upset that the spouse is leaving; this person becomes disoriented. Often I have had to make sure that someone stayed with such an individual to prevent something precipitous from happening. Initially someone needs to be constantly present to provide boundaries for rational behavior.

This feeling of alienation affects all facets of a person's life (see Fig. 3.8).

"When Jim told me he had never loved me and could never love me, he destroyed my self-image," reveals Bonnie. "I lived in a fog for two years. I concentrated on three things: being a good teacher; being a good mother to my children; and doing my work in the junior church. Yet I would go on crying jags and insist, 'I'm not worthy for anyone to love.' "

A highly effective executive may be suddenly paralyzed after being rejected by his wife through divorce. For a year or more he is barely "there" on the job, and he provides little effective input. A college professor "taught" for one whole year, but he cannot remember any of his students or what happened in his classes.

Fig. 3.8. Alienation

The following definition of *alienation* is taken from an article, "Schools for Fearlessness and Freedom," written by Eugene Mc-Creary. It covers the subject admirably.

Alienation is the name for the weakening of the ties of community and family, for the loss of creative enjoyment in work, for uncertainty in all things, for dependency and the confusing and contradictory expectations of economic and social life, for weakened personal integrity, for a sense of hopelessness, meaninglessness, uselessness, and irrelevance, for conformity in culture and politics, for a loss of faith, for the separation of man from his natural roots, for the decay of love. The alienated are unable to realize or define themselves. The dimensions of alienation are a generalized anxiety, shifting from object to object, and a confused and debilitated sense of human identity and personal responsibility. The alienated stand as ready pawns for strange new faiths, for excitements strong enough to divert them, for cruel myths or polarized evil and virtue, and for a shifting of responsibility to others.

What can you do to combat your feelings of alienation, regain a healthy self-image, and once again become an effective, functioning adult? You can recognize that you are not alone; God is with you and He "knows the secrets of the heart" (Ps. 44:21) and everything else about you (see Ps. 139:1–4). You can realize that you are important to God and that you have His love: "God is love, and the one who abides in love abides in God, and God abides in him" (1 John 4:16). And you can remember that you have a new self "renewed to a true knowledge according to the image of the One who created" you (Col. 3:10).

Once two individuals have suffered all the pain and hurt that leads up to and follows a divorce, can their relationship ever be restored to the friendship level? Can new limits of harmony be established between former marriage partners? More than 250 couples have now participated in my reconciliation seminars and classes, and the evidence is in that friendship can be restored even when one or both of the spouses have remarried. And remarriage to each other is possible when neither has remarried and both are willing to start again at the acquaintanceship level, move through the friendship level, and establish a new relationship. That is why I have taken the time to write this book. John and Judy, Jim and Bonnie, are but two of the couples whose experiences will reveal what can happen to you.

The Onset of Disharmony

If you were to sit down with a piece of paper and list in sequence the events that contributed most to the growth of disharmony in your marriage, would you be able to do it? Certainly you would! We all have a way of remembering rather clearly the disagreements, the verbal battles, and the confrontations over events that triggered disharmony. Those were the times when we bumped up against the limits of harmony or we actually broke through into disharmony.

For some, the onset of disharmony preceded the wedding. It may have even been over who was to be invited to the wedding. In your mind you pictured a nice, quiet wedding with thirty to thirty-five guests. But your fiancée's family required a larger event; anything less than two hundred guests would have been an inadequate size for proper community recognition.

You went along with it after a running argument because you decided the issue was not important enough to disturb future marital harmony. Yet you did not really come to terms with the differing level of expectations, and the disagreement became the seed of disharmony.

For you, a party consisted of two to three couples. You felt more comfortable in a small group because that was how your parents entertained. However, your wife wanted to have eight to ten couples at a time: she pictured you as the life of the party and the master of the art of barbecuing chicken and steaks—just like her father had been. Your inability to perform at that level brought on the arguments that eventually pushed you both to the outer limits of disharmony soon after the wedding.

For Jim, the issue that contributed to many arguments was orderliness and neatness in the home. He cannot tolerate a trail of clothes, shoes, and books throughout the house. He is irritated by having to pick up after people.

"Jim is a neatnik," says Bonnie, "and I'm a teacher. When I get home, I am tired and don't have the energy to get after the children, let alone embark on getting things cleaned up."

For Bonnie, the issue concerned Jim's inability to show affection. She received a lot of love and affection as well as spiritual support in her first marriage. She expected Jim to provide the same warm, loving environment, and she was deeply disappointed when he couldn't seem to do that.

"My son from my first marriage would hug Jim because he was warm and affectionate like his father. Jim would accept it, but would not hug back. In his family, the men did not show affection. I missed the affection my first husband had given me in my relationship with Jim," says Bonnie.

What Bonnie did not realize was that despite the wedding, Jim still did not feel any affection for her. Her expectations only placed more of a burden on Jim, who kept wondering why he had fallen for the white knight role. Because neither of them met the other's expectations, the seeds of disharmony sprouted into giant trees of disagreement.

Disharmony resulting from unmet expectations *before* marriage only increases when there are other unfulfilled expectations *after* marriage. Jim liked his wife to have some spunk, to take initiative, and to demonstrate aggressiveness. That was out of character for Bonnie, since she had been married once and found happiness in a submissive role with a loving, caring husband. Yet Jim kept hoping that as she gained experience as a teacher, as she grew older, she would demonstrate more of a take-charge nature.

Jim discovered too late that Bonnie really had the inner character to become spunky. His lack of emotional support made her so insecure that she decided to remain submissive rather than risk losing him. After the trauma and alienation of a divorce, when her children provided that loving response, she blossomed into her own person—something Jim found most attractive when he considered reconciliation.

Another contributing factor to disharmony is the lessening of quality time together. It may start with the husband's climb up the executive ladder, immersion in a position as a traveling sales representative, or into a professional-level job such as minister, counselor, doctor, or media specialist. The early years demand an incredible amount of effort and time in most vocations, yet those are also often the wife's child-bearing years.

When a husband concentrates on doing his job and a wife concentrates on raising their children, their time together becomes shorter and shorter. They are more preoccupied with keeping up with events at the office and in the home than with building in-depth levels of communication. Consequently one day the husband discovers he is emotionally attracted to an associate with whom he spends a lot of time on the job. The wife finds her association with a man at a church-related or community outreach is more exciting than times with her husband.

In the growth of friendship and relationships, the controlling factor is accumulated time spent together. If that is the case in the dating relationship, why should it be any different in a marriage?

When a couple do not spend enough quality time together, they basically lose track of each other. Oh, they still see each other at mealtimes and on weekends, and they have some idea where the other is geographically, but they miss learning about each other's internal growth.

Open lines of communication are vital to a harmonious marriage. An old Chinese proverb states, "Though conversing face to face, their hearts have a thousand miles between them." Some couples may think they are communicating when they converse face to face, but that is not always the case, as the proverb makes clear. Couples must do more than converse; they have to communicate so that they can bring their hearts closer together and thus strengthen their marital relationship.

Separation—The Normal Direction of Marriage

In order to keep your car running smoothly, you must have a routine of preventive maintenance. In order to keep your marriage running smoothly, you must follow a similar policy. Work hard to keep the hours you spend together from deteriorating to zero. The time you spend together is part of this "preventive maintenance." You cannot allow your relationship to run its natural course, or it will suffer from the neglect (see Fig. 4.1, which shows the tendency for intimacy to decline as time goes by). You should always keep in mind that separation is the normal direction of marriage, so your efforts are to thwart that drift and keep your relationship on the more harmonious course leading to togetherness.

Many couples who have been married for twenty to thirty years find themselves back at the friendship level. Some choose to get a friendly divorce and remain friends for many more years. Others are able to rekindle the fire and restore the relationship. Marriage Encounter and other programs that give couples large doses of extended quality time alone are very helpful. Such programs also stress the need for every couple to evaluate the priorities in their relationships.

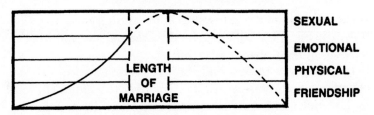

Fig. 4.1. Relationship After the Wedding

Figure 4.1. The two vertical lines represent an indefinite time period. Today's marriage averages seven years, with the center space open-ended for the shorter or longer ones that have reached a plateau. The solid line represents growth from the friendship level to emotional togetherness in marriage as steps in the progress of a marriage. The broken line represents regression to the friendship stage. Sexual activity may continue, but it is not an expression of oneness. Instead it satisfies a physical desire like an occasional ice-cream cone.

A most helpful book is *Secrets of a Growing Marriage* by Roger and Donna Vann, which provides interaction questions for weekend retreats for marriage renewal and growth. Also, *Ten Dates for Mates* by Dave and Claudia Arp is a useful book.

No Time Together

Marriages may degenerate to the friendship level when one spouse finds activity away from the home more satisfying than time spent at home with a marriage partner. Typically, women will get involved in church activities, while men will find reasons to work overtime or stop at a bar or the softball diamond. At times, a husband will find alternative activity at the church, not recognizing his motives for doing so. Whatever activity robs a couple of adequate time together to develop a context for understanding each other is a threat to their marriage.

In Bonnie's case, she loved her time leading junior church and being involved in other church activities. She had made a personal commitment to Jesus Christ as her Savior years earlier and found the fellowship in the church enriching. She was growing spiritually despite the inner tensions of her deteriorating relationship with Jim.

Jim did not understand Bonnie's commitment to the church. In fact, he resented it. Although he went to church, he had not made a faith commitment, and he couldn't be bothered with active church involvement. When he and Bonnie talked, it was at the trivial level of "Where have you been?" or "What are you doing?" instead of "How are you feeling?" or "What new insights are you gaining about life?"

Since they did not share intimately, Jim never did understand Bonnie's motivation for her extensive involvement in the church, nor did he recognize her growth as a person as a result. So, he found himself getting emotionally involved with another woman, who seemed so much more interesting than his wife.

The harmony of a marriage is seriously disrupted when a couple does not take time to share deeply with each other. They do not really know each other, so they persistently misread each other's motivation, their expressed goals in life, and even their actions.

All of us need a context, or a set of shared experiences, if we are to understand each other. Obviously, there is no way to accumulate such experiences if we spend little or no quality time together. The more experiences and communication about them that we share, the better we understand each other.

Remember when you were in high school or college and wrote exams or term papers? Most of us discovered early on that making passing grades did not merely mean doing our homework well and cramming for exams. Equally important was learning how the teachers or professors functioned, what kind of information they considered important, and what standards they used to mark our papers. The context informed us about how to feed back the content, yet we could not develop that context until we had attended the class for several months (three to five hours a week) and until we had gone through a whole series of trial runs (the initial tests and first essays).

Too Many Misunderstandings

Inability to respond properly to a marriage partner's feelings because of lack of context often results in emotional explosions, which may coincide with an outright disagreement or a disappointment over unfulfilled expectations. If these emotional outbursts carry one or both partners to the outer limits of harmony enough times, it is easy to rationalize that the marriage is dead.

The problem of misreading each other's motives and actions may be compounded by the partners' going beyond the limits of individual and family goals and aspirations. In today's affluent society, these goals can change rapidly or assume various forms unless husband and wife spend sufficient time discussing them and reach an understanding about them. Disagreements over these goals can easily develop into major areas of disharmony.

Susan had not completed her sophomore year in college when she met Gene, who was handsome, self-assured, and goal oriented. She felt she was ready to marry and begin a family, even though she knew she would have to quit school. After their marriage Gene completed graduate theological work and joined a major Christian organization. He served on the board of elders at his church and often filled the pulpit during the pastor's absence. He was promoted and soon achieved a significant executive position, working long, hard hours.

He and Susan had three children, and she filled the role of model mother. She made most of the clothes for the children and kept an immaculate house. At church she became active in Sunday school and in the club for young girls. Yet her lack of a college degree haunted her. She began taking classes for credit that were offered on television; she got up early several days a week to tune in.

When the children reached their teens, Susan gained an interest in physical fitness. She not only enjoyed the activity, but she became so proficient she was appointed an aerobics teacher. This venture introduced her to a whole new set of women. They bubbled over with the new feminist objectives. Hardly realizing it, Susan developed a real dissatisfaction with her lifestyle. She wasn't about to remain a stick-in-the-mud with her husband. Despite the clearly defined Christian convictions she held as a teen and as a young mother, she shifted into a more permissive lifestyle. Eventually she moved in with a younger man she had met in her new environment.

Though many factors are at work when a person makes such a shift, the lack of quality time with a superbusy spouse can contribute significantly to the onset of disharmony.

Though children often hold a couple together during stressful times, they may also contribute to disharmony. Unless couples spend some quality time together discussing and agreeing on goals to achieve with their children, on ways to discipline and on how much freedom to give teens, disagreements over these matters can be a constant source of disharmony.

Jean was raised in an extremely strict home and church. The list of don'ts was always longer than the list of do's. She considered that environment a negative factor, but she instinctively sought the same kind of control over her children, since she knew nothing else.

Her husband Al grew up in a much less oppressive environment. Within certain agreed-upon limits, he had a lot of freedom. His nature was like that of his father, who tended to let disciplinary situations develop over a period of time before he became upset enough to take action. Thus Jean's resentment would build as she pondered Al's "failure" to take action when the children "needed" discipline. Though she held to their agreement not to air their child-raising disagreements in front of the children, Jean would focus on this particular subject whenever she became depressed for one reason or another. Al found himself withdrawing at such times, since any attempt at explanation of his approach caused her to intensify her tirade.

How Far Can Things Go?

We have seen in Figure 4.1 that marriage can drift back to friendship, but what happens next? Just as there are steps going up, there are steps going down, and Figure 4.2 shows the four steps going down: anger, bitterness, pugnaciousness, and death.

The anger here is different from that of simple disharmony. It is the everyday intensity that grows without resolu-

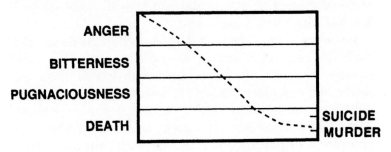

Fig. 4.2. Steps Down in a Relationship

tion. As this anger intensifies and begins to alter the personality, it hardens into bitterness. In some instances this process can take a few months to solidify, but in others it may take a few years. By the time the couple reach the next step, they may be throwing things or physically abusing each other. Remember the couple who exchange their children on the steps of the police department? The sundering of an emotional commitment is not a smooth affair.

Let me ask again, How far can things go? Many of you feel that you have been all the way: suffering physical abuse, obtaining restraining orders, having the door kicked in or the furniture destroyed. Yet that is only the beginning, not the end. One of every four murders occurs within the family unit, and half of these are between spouses. The end is death! The Scriptures say the wages of sin is death, and there are many sins in the process of divorce.

Death comes in two forms: one spouse kills the other, or lacking the strength to do that, one spouse commits suicide in order to put an end to the pain and misery. Look back at Figure 3.8 in Chapter Three; the alienation described there creates the environment for these irrational responses. The death of the marriage is now complete. It has run full course from friendship to marriage, back to friendship, and then downward to death. Figure 4.3 provides an overall view of the total process. It also allows you to evaluate where you are and where you want to go.

If you are at Line 1, now is the time to stop the downward cycle. You can choose to allow the cycle to continue or to determine to rebuild the relationship with lots of hours together and just plain hard work. The choice is up to you.

Even if you are at the point of Line 2, you have hope. Many couples you will read about later will confirm that you can be reconciled. You must deal with your own bitterness and apply huge doses of forgiveness and self-control.

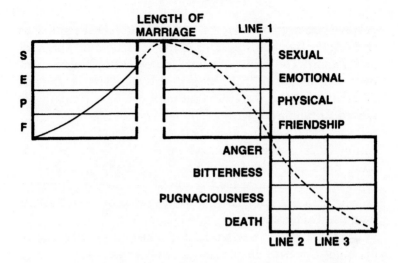

Fig. 4.3. Death of a Marriage

This zone is critical. If a couple has not separated to this point, the marriage may be turned around before the next step is reached. The only time a couple should be counseled to separate is when physical abuse has occurred. Any earlier separation would reduce the time they can spend together and would thus contribute to the death of the relationship, but waiting longer could risk physical harm that could be difficult to reconcile later.

Line 3 forms the barrier to the ultimate destruction of the relationship by death. Severe guidelines and actions are justified at this point, but you still have hope with counsel, spiritual growth, and emotional maturity. (In Chapter Eleven I give some practical step by step guidelines that have been proved to provide hope and motivation to return to harmony from the near death of the marriage.)

Have you ever wondered what it would have been like to sit in on the family discussions in the household of Abraham and Sarah? The biblical record notes their disagreement over a stepchild. Both Ishmael and Isaac were the sons of Abraham, but they had different mothers. Sarah harshly attacked Abraham for letting Ishmael and his mother, Hagar, remain with them after Isaac was born. "Now Sarah saw the son of Hagar the Egyptian, whom she had borne to Abraham, mocking. Therefore she said to Abraham, 'Drive out this maid and her son, for the son of this maid shall not be an heir with my son Isaac.' And the matter distressed Abraham greatly because of his son" (Gen. 21:9–11).

Abraham saw the potential for constant disharmony in his home. He was unsure about what to do until the Lord provided directions. Even though the action seemed cruel and inhuman, Abraham could send Hagar and Ishmael away into the desert because of the Lord's clear directions, which provided a perspective he could not see.

The new perspective that many of us need is found in the apostle Paul's directions to the Ephesians. Paul wrote, "Nevertheless let each individual among you also love his own wife even as himself; and let the wife see to it that she respect her husband" (Eph. 5:33). When the husband genuinely loves his wife, it is most difficult for her to move him to the outer limits of harmony by attacking him in an argument. He is more likely to look for ways to defuse an argument than to attempt to get even.

That is what happened with Jim and Bonnie. When Jim reached the end of his personal resources as a divorced single, he turned himself over to God.

"I decided I had to take a look at my life. I promised the Lord if He would help me I would try to be reconciled to

Bonnie. It was clear to me that was what He wanted," says Jim.

Once he developed that perspective, the potential for reconciliation became much greater. His commitment to God's perspective on marriage helped him turn disagreement with Bonnie into a stepping stone to new levels of harmony.

Garth's experience was somewhat different from Jim's. As a marriage counselor, Garth had plenty of advice for other couples, but he did not seem to have the proper perspective on what could save his own marriage. Divorce shattered his professional confidence, destroyed his self-image, and set him on the path of alcoholism. When he had lost everything, including the ability to hold a job, he did what Jim did: He turned his life over to God and went back to church. There he discovered a group of Christian alcoholics, where he gained acceptance and understanding.

"I am absolutely certain that if I had given my marriage the priorities God gives it, He would have helped me save it. Now my wife has remarried and the opportunity is gone," he says. His three-piece pinstripe suit is testimony to his new ability to hold a significant job, but his loneliness is testimony to a lost opportunity of remarriage. His only hope now is to bring back harmony and friendship between himself and his ex-wife.

What were the areas of disagreement in your relationship with your former spouse? Can you now pinpoint with greater clarity the kinds of reactions that escalated disagreements? Were they really worth exceeding the limits of harmony and getting a divorce?

As we have discussed, working toward reconciliation will not be an easy task. It will require a lot of hard work and a lot of honest answers to a lot of painful questions such as these. Let's move on to the next chapter and examine your potential for reconciliation.

Considering the Potential

If you have read this far, you may be in one of three categories: You are separated, you are divorced, or you hope to help yourself or someone else headed in that direction. Now you are ready to move beyond an analysis of what went wrong and why the instances of disharmony jumped off the chart to a consideration of the factors affecting the potential for reconciliation.

I want to be perfectly honest with you. For most of you, reconciliation will never mean remarriage to the person you came to dislike, dare I say *loathe*? Maybe *fear* is a better word in some cases. Perhaps your former spouse has remarried, and you feel sorry for the new spouse—even if she or he stole your ex from you. But at least you do not have to consider remarriage to that person, and that is a relief because Deuteronomy 24:4 reads, "Then her former husband who sent her away is not allowed to take her again to be his wife, since she has been defiled; for that is an abomination before the LORD, and you shall not bring sin on the land which the LORD your God gives you as an inheritance."

Some of you left behind a truly unstable, irresponsible person. Only a miracle of grace on the part of a forgiving God could ever change that person into someone more desirable as a marriage partner.

So what am I trying to accomplish by urging you to consider reconciliation? The primary goal of reconciliation is friendship. I can't repeat that too often. If you can bring back harmony into your relationship, you will be able to treat your ex as you would any other person. Getting rid of your anger and bitterness will help you and everyone else concerned.

You see, many people move into a new relationship after a divorce without ever considering reconciliation. Yet that new relationship is tough enough to develop and deepen without bringing along heavy baggage of anger and hostility. Those unreconciled ex's may pop up at the most unexpected times.

Let's say you pull yourself together, and someone comes into your life and wants to build a relationship. Since your ex left the marriage, you feel free to start a new life. But suddenly your ex bounces back into your life and wants to reconcile with you. As you have been moving toward the outer limits of the reconciliation cycle, your ex has been moving toward the center.

At this point you are probably uncertain about what to do and about how the course of your life will be affected by what you decide to do. But you decide to give it a try. You break up your new relationship and get back to the line of reconciliation, ready to reconcile with your ex. However, by that time, your ex has met someone else and has moved toward the outer limits of the cycle. So, you wait a few weeks or months and get tired of waiting for your ex to move back toward the line of reconciliation. You meet someone else and get serious. Then the whole process starts over again. Your ex shows up again and is ready for reconciliation. You both keep cycling back to the reconciliation point, but you are just a few months out of sync with each other. Figure 5.1 is a graphic representation of this process.

Let's say you have entered a new relationship and have be-

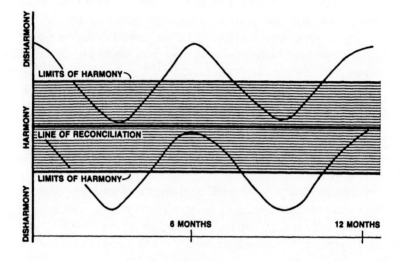

Fig. 5.1. Cycles of Reconciliation

come engaged. Then your ex comes along and wants to reconcile, so you break off your engagement only to have your ex move out of your life again. You are left once more at some point of the cycle that is out of sync with your ex. Maybe you have both remarried but your ex wants to get together again. Your ex is in an unhappy new marriage, and he or she feels your new one is not that great either. Believe it or not, this is a common situation. The cycles of reconciliation are not limited by divorce or remarriage.

Why wait to reconcile with your ex? Wouldn't you be better off to effect reconciliation before you start another relationship? You can avoid a lot of complications that way.

Let's discuss some of the factors affecting the potential for reconciliation.

Preserving Family Relationships

Reconciliation at times gains significance from family relationships. My parents were separated for twenty-six or twenty-seven years, but they never divorced. I can remember that as a teen I would go with the family to see relatives in the Midwest and my father would visit us there. We would have a big family get-together, and he would introduce his "wife" and the children he had not lived with for many years.

What made that possible? My parents had reconciled so they could be around each other and be comfortable in the extended family environment. It had taken some time—the first time together as a family was quite uncomfortable, but later they managed well.

Taking God Seriously

For some people, a new or revitalized relationship with God opens the door to take His commands seriously.

Remember Jim and Bonnie? Jim had never genuinely liked and respected Bonnie because she was not assertive enough. And Bonnie had grown to really dislike Jim because of what he had done to her in getting a divorce. Yet once Jim committed himself to Jesus Christ and accepted His forgiveness, he decided to do something about his estrangement from Bonnie.

"I decided the best thing I could do was to become friends—to open the door and see what could happen. But we were spinning our wheels until we met Jim Talley and agreed to the friendship covenant," says Jim. (Friendship instruction and the friendship covenant will be explained in Chapter Eleven. Then you will see how important it is to spend this time together.)

As Jim and Bonnie purposefully spent time together, they

suddenly realized they were beginning to like each other. And because they had not remarried and were both still free, they could move to the relationship level and re-establish their home. Yet even if they had stayed at the friendship level, the heat created by their dislike of each other would have been eliminated.

Most of you need to stop and ask yourself, *Do I want another go at the same kind of relationship I had?* If you are honest with yourself, you will say, "No!" Then why not consider the potential of reconciling with your ex on a new basis? The new basis is a more mature, more stable, and more effective you.

The Scriptures tell us how to become new: "If any man is in Christ, he is a new creature; the old things have passed away; behold, new things have come" (2 Cor. 5:17). Believing in Jesus and accepting Him, we put aside the old self and put on the new self (see Eph. 4:21–24). Becoming a new person will help you build a new relationship. In addition, if you learn from the past, live in the present, and plan for the future, you will be taking the right steps toward a more solid relationship committed to taking God's commands seriously.

Reconciliation Cycle

The biggest factor affecting the potential for reconciliation is the recurring cycle of reconciliation God has built into our relationships. Once you have progressed from friendship to relationship a new dynamic called "homeostasis" takes hold. We discussed this briefly in an earlier chapter.

You have developed a comfort zone where you both feel at home, even though the relationship is far from perfect. When you are close together, you are never aware of homeostasis because it doesn't really do anything to you. When you start to pull apart, it seems to dig into you. Its effects are ever so slight at first, but the farther apart you get, the more forcefully it works to pull you together.

Here is how homeostasis can work. You may each be on the outer limits of harmony, and you may not be speaking to each other. Although this can be an extremely painful point, there is no intense anger or bitterness. Then the constant pressure toward reconciliation may move one of you toward the center, which releases the pressure from the other person, and both of you return to the center.

When a couple leave the limits of harmony, the homeostasis is broken, and all kinds of negative emotions result. Although both of you will feel free to leave the situation, there is a certain amount of attachment, which represents a certain potential for reconciliation.

The Apostle Paul's Experience

Remember the disagreement the legendary missionary pioneer, the apostle Paul, had with Barnabas over John Mark? When the church at Antioch sent Paul and Barnabas on the first missionary journey, Barnabas took along a trainee, his nephew John Mark. They had some exciting experiences together on the island of Cyprus, and they had the kind of success that knits a team together.

Yet toward the end of their stay on Cyprus, something apparently happened between Paul and John Mark. Not even his uncle could prevent John Mark from leaving the advance party. Luke stated simply, "Now Paul and his companions put out to sea from Paphos and came to Perga in Pamphylia; and John left them and returned to Jerusalem" (Acts 13:13).

Clearly, the outer limits of harmony had been breached by John Mark and the apostle Paul. When Paul and Barnabas were about to begin their second journey, their relationship became severely strained over the issue of taking John Mark. "And there arose such a sharp disagreement that they separated from one another, and Barnabas took Mark with him and sailed away to Cyprus. But Paul chose Silas and departed" (Acts 15:39–40).

Imagine these two Spirit-led missionaries reaching the outer limits of harmony and exploding beyond that because of a disagreement over this young man. The nurturing nature of Barnabas, whose name means "son of consolation," turned away from the less sympathetic Paul, and another beautiful relationship was broken.

Yet the love that God had poured into the heart of the apostle Paul won out in the end. The effects of homeostasis brought John Mark back into the relationship. He once again became "useful to me," to use Paul's words. In fact, Paul recommended that the Colossians welcome John Mark if he should visit them (see Col. 4:10). Paul wrote an even greater commendation when he included John Mark among those few Jews who "have proved to be an encouragement to me" (Col. 4:11). Homeostasis thus is a very positive force that increases the potential for reconciliation.

Children Want Normal Relations

If you have been through a divorce and you end up with the children, you will quickly learn about their powerful desire to put the family back together again. If they see that there is no apparent chance at reconciliation between you and your ex, the first person who appears to have the potential to make the family whole again will be subjected to tremendous pressure.

Here is what happens. Susan's divorce is final. Enough time has gone by for her to become functional again. The two children recognize that the father is gone. The family as they knew it is dead.

Along comes Henry to pick up Susan for their first date. She is dressing as he arrives, and six-year-old Dick answers the door. Henry asks, "Is your mother ready?" Dick looks Henry over and says, "Almost. Are you going to marry her tonight or tomorrow?"

As a parent in that situation, you need to prepare anybody who comes into your life for those kinds of questions and comments. That is not a reflection of your feelings about the relationship, but it does reflect the pressure children bring to bear.

Single or Remarried

Another factor affecting the potential for reconciliation is whether either of you has remarried. Once you are divorced, the easiest way for you to fill the emptiness is to get into a new relationship. The number of divorced singles makes it fairly easy to find someone also trying to ease the pain of loneliness.

What most new singles do not recognize is that the alienation they experience immediately after separation and divorce is a major hindrance to a new relationship. It's like the marathon runner who has had surgery. Recovery is slow, even with good care. That person does not get up and run twenty laps around the hospital corridor the day after surgery.

In the same way the new single is not ready to jump into a new relationship without going through the "hospital" stay after the emotional surgery of divorce. Allowing time for an adequate recovery means an individual hasn't entered into a second (or third) relationship or marriage! This time also permits the former mate to cycle back into a reconciliation pattern, vastly increasing the chances of reconciliation to at least the friendship level.

When John finally had to live alone after Judy "booted"

him out, he dated several women to glory in his new freedom. He found them all unsatisfactory, and he finally focused his attention on his motorcycle. The thought of entering any relationship became totally unappealing to him.

"My motorcycle became my idol," he says.

One day he was involved in a motorcycle accident that nearly cost him his life. Though he walked away with only bruises and scrapes, he realized how close he had come to death.

"Judy had given me the 'Four Spiritual Laws' booklet when I left. Though I normally keep nothing, for some reason I had kept this for two years. I found it the night of the accident. After reading it, I prayed, 'Lord, if this is real, I want it.' The Lord met me that night and I went forward in church the next Sunday," he recalls.

Judy saw the potential for reconciliation immediately when she saw John going to the front of the church to publicly affirm his decision to follow Christ. When he made the commitment to Christ, they were both ready for reconciliation since neither of them had remarried, but had taken the time to recover.

Though the reconciliation took a lot more effort than they initially expected, John and Judy have now been remarried for more than six years. Imagine what would have happened if either had married someone else during their period of alienation. For them, the recovery period of separation and, finally, divorce had been six years.

As the years go by, the potential for reconciliation declines. Either or both may marry again. They may move worlds apart geographically. Closely held bitterness has a way of crowding out potential for reconciliation. Thus it becomes vital to be available for reconciliation when your ex cycles back into your life looking for some semblance of normalcy in the relationship.

By now some of you may be saying, "Those are all great ideas, but how can I ever get hold of my feelings enough to maximize the potential for reconciliation?" Bonnie felt that way until during one seminar she heard me say, "Love is an act of the will."

"No way was I ready to accept that, not the way I felt about Jim," she confesses. "Yet I found out he was right."

Why am I right in that assertion? The apostle Paul in 1 Corinthians 13 lets us in on the secret in his poetic expression of the nature of love. Each of us would do well to incorporate each attribute into our behavior.

Love is patient. You do not lose control the first time there is a problem.

Love is kind. It is not envious. You do not retaliate even when your ex is nasty. You do not envy others doing well or elements in another's relationship that you do not have in yours.

Love is not boastful. You do not brag about how well you are doing now and about how poorly your ex is doing.

Love is humble. You are willing to accept yourself in whatever situation you are in and to be content with that.

Love is gracious. You communicate in a kind and tactful way.

Love is not demanding. You can accept the situation when things do not always go your way or when you do not always get what you want.

Love is not revengeful. Though revenge is a natural reaction, you have to come to grips with the damage it does. You cannot ever say, "I don't want to get back; I just want to get even."

Love is forgiving. You have the ability to consciously erase those things in your past that stir up anger and hatred. You learn to forget them and go on as you let the Holy Spirit control your thoughts. Forgetting does not mean you erase them from your mind or memory, but it means you no longer react emotionally to bad memories as they pop up.

Love is helpful and is willing to respond in concern for the other person. You do not gloat over the misfortune of your ex; you express honest sympathy.

Love is not deceiving. You do not consciously try to deceive or fault another by saying things that are not really true. Nor do you try to hide things, lie about them, or take them when they do not belong to you.

Love is not repulsed. That is a tough concept to deal with. When you give something and it is not accepted, you continue to offer it. No matter how the other person reacts to you, you keep on loving. This is vital to any move toward reconciliation.

Love is trusting and hopeful. You look for the positive things in life and in others. Love is forbearing and triumphant. You overcome anger, bitterness, and frustration, and you continue to love.

As I look at God's standard, I see a lot of hard work. Love is not so much a warm puppy-like feeling inside your life, the feeling of being on a cloud of ecstasy, as it is an ongoing process of *doing* and *acting* in love in order *to be* in love. Unfortunately, in our society most of us have been taught only to feel love, so once that feeling is gone we give up and then we wonder why things did not work out.

If you want to maximize the potential for the right kind of love, you need the power of the One who is love: "For God has not given us a spirit of timidity, but of power and love and discipline" (2 Tim. 1:7). Only as the living Christ lives inside you and expresses Himself in power in you will you be able to love as we have discussed here. We are told that nothing can separate us from the love of Christ, but in all things we "overwhelmingly conquer through Him who loved us" (Rom. 8:35–37).

In Ephesians 1:15 the apostle Paul commended the Ephesians for their "love for all the saints." He followed that up by introducing them to the "surpassing greatness of His power toward us who believe" (v. 19). This power is available to all who are filled with the Holy Spirit, who represents Christ in us: "The love of God has been poured out within our hearts through the Holy Spirit who was given to us" (Rom. 5:5). If you are filled with this love and power, your potential for reconciliation will be greatly enhanced.

Regaining Control

When are you ready to move toward reconciliation? Does wanting to be reconciled qualify you? Or do you need to wait a certain period of time?

One of the most important things you can do in preparation for reconciliation is to regain control of your life. Typically, the newly divorced person will experience alienation and will be emotionally out of control for several months and, in some cases, for as long as a year. During that adjustment period, there is a fairly predictable pattern of excess in several areas. If you have fallen prey to one (or more) of these excesses, you need to recognize what has happened to you in this area, and you need to begin to regain control of it.

Out of Control

Recently I was approached by a man in his forties who wanted help in reconciling with his wife. She had moved home with her parents in another state.

"Do you have a stable job?" I asked.

"No," he said, "but we can get a house, and she can work while I continue looking for a job."

"No way will I help you reconcile with your wife," I told him, "until you have held a job long enough to demonstrate you are in control of your life. Only when you are financially responsible will I help you be reconciled with your wife."

Though he has been divorced for more than a year, Ben (not his real name) still has not regained control over his life. He wanted to be reconciled for the purpose of sexual satisfaction, not to contribute to his former spouse's sense of security or to build a harmonious relationship with her.

Sex

One of the most obvious areas in which a new single needs to regain control is sexual. Not surprisingly, 90 per cent of all divorced people cycle in and out of the bar and bedroom scene—and that includes Christians. They become morally irrational, go to a bar (where they may never have been before), meet someone, and have a physical relationship. They may repeat this pattern over and over again, or they may spend a weekend with someone they hardly know, or they may go through a series of live-in relationships.

In Figure 6.1 we can see the complexities of sexual activity outside marriage and the effects on three families. The husband in Couple 1 has an affair with the wife in Couple 2 (the first affair). In response, the wife in Couple 1 becomes involved with the husband in Couple 3 (the second affair). The husband in Couple 2 gets involved with someone else (the third affair), and the wife in Couple 3 meets someone new (the fourth affair). Some of these people profess to be Christians and are members of the church. I have known of real life situations just like this.

It is not as though these people do not know what is right. Even the person who is not a Christian instinctively knows that, for the apostle Paul wrote, after listing moral excesses, "And, although they know the ordinance of God, that those who practice such things are worthy of death, they not only

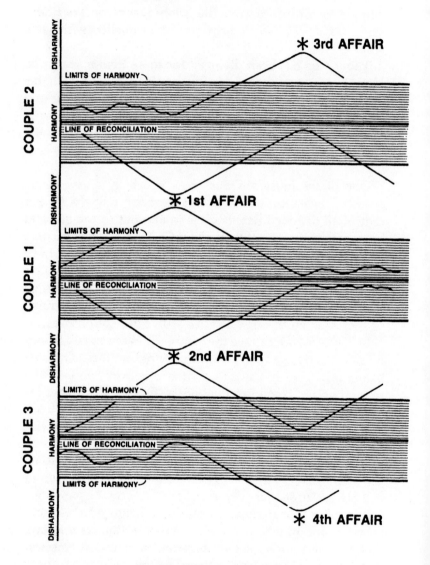

Fig. 6.1. Cycles of Complexities

do the same, but also give hearty approval to those who practice them" (Rom. 1:32).

From this passage it is clear that the sexually active person needs a change in attitude. I find that when people begin to adopt God's attitude, to say, "No, I shouldn't do that," they are beginning to regain control. Only as they get back to their moral commitments can they re-establish control over the sexual area of life. Relying upon the Holy Spirit for help in this area is wise: "Walk by the Spirit, and you will not carry out the desire of the flesh" (Gal. 5:16).

Romance

Some men become caught up in the quest for romance. These are the men who wanted romantic and responsive wives, but they were unwilling to do what was needed to ring the bells of romance in their marriage and give their wives any special treatment. After they are divorced, they suddenly remember all the thoughtful things they did as young men.

Let's look at an example. Our typical suitor bathes, shaves, puts on cologne (for the first time in ten years), orders flowers, makes reservations, and takes his new friend out for a great evening of dining and dancing. He takes her home and feels really good about how things went. He has done none of those things with his wife in twenty years of marriage, but he wonders why his new friend was such a delightful companion. With a little effort like that, he and his ex-wife could remain on very friendly terms.

Although losing control in this area may not be as serious in its effects as losing control in other areas, men who are continuously searching for the "perfect" romantic situation and partner may never settle down to a serious, long-term relationship. They need to regain control so that they can view life more realistically and take advantage of opportunities they have to reconcile with their ex's.

Finances

Another area in which people need to regain control is in finances. The wife may consider her husband responsible for all of the bills after separation. She will go on a shopping spree and use up all the credit on every credit card. The husband, on the other hand, may recognize that he can stick his wife with the bills, so he loads the cards to the hilt before she has a chance to cancel the joint accounts.

Many wives today are paying off debts accumulated by their husbands before legal action separated financial obligations. Recently a couple was forced into foreclosure because creditors trying to recoup their losses attached the wife's salary and that of her new husband. Her former husband incurred tremendous debts after they separated. That is why a legal separation is so important: It removes the community property liabilities from both parties.

Another out-of-control reaction is typified by Eric (not his real name), who has a good job as well as investments in real estate. When his divorce became final, he sold one of his properties and purchased a luxury Mercedes-Benz coupe. It sits in his garage most of the time. He did not need it; he bought it only as an expression of his new freedom.

Another drain on your finances can be fees of counselors or lawyers. Counseling often runs from seventy-five to ninety dollars an hour, and two or three appointments a week can quickly exhaust a savings account. The rush to get a divorce, which can involve disputed property settlements or custody battles for children, can be very costly.

Beauty and Fitness

Many newly single women are in a hurry to appear physically beautiful. They will sign up for aerobics and a reducing program and then invest in a new wardrobe. I know women who have been overweight for years, who seemed to have lost all interest in themselves, but they get a divorce and lose all the excess weight. They suddenly become sports nuts and get totally involved in all kinds of activities—racquetball, volleyball, jogging, and tennis. I call this "the sports excessive syndrome."

The new activities, new diets, and new wardrobes seem to be all they can think about or talk about. Although a certain interest in these matters is normal and healthy, anything carried to an extreme can prevent the individuals from having balanced lives. Regaining control in this area can help them regain that necessary balance.

Travel

Some newly divorced people go on a travel binge. They go to the Holy Land, Europe, the Caribbean, Hawaii, or Japan, or all of these places. If they don't have that kind of money, they might become conference-ites. They will go to every conference and retreat they know about—and some they do not know about. It seems that every weekend they are at some singles conference, trying to get their lives back together again while spending exorbitant amounts of money.

They need to realize that they cannot escape their problems in a new location and they cannot become "new" persons by traveling constantly. Sometimes their travel habits only compound their problems because when they are at home, they feel no better or no different from how they felt before they left.

Once people recognize the areas that are out of control, they can take steps to regain control. And that will not be easy in many cases. Some sacrifices or changes will probably be required, and neither alternative is attractive to most people.

The B-B Approach

Instead of spending money, the divorced person needs to balance the budget. That's why I call this the "B-B approach." Getting control of the spending may be a new experience for some men, because in about 60 per cent of the cases the wife did the family accounting. In most cases, the newly divorced need to burn their credit cards, cut overhead to the bone, and even sell off unneeded cars. A garage sale may be necessary in some instances. Anything to begin balancing the financial records will be helpful.

Most couples today have come to depend on a two-income lifestyle. Yet even with two incomes, they barely manage to run a one-overhead household. Separated, they suddenly have two overheads because of two households, and a negative cash flow is the outcome. So, when you separate it is important to downgrade yourself financially as quickly as possible.

What does this mean? For most of you it will mean moving into a less expensive house or apartment, reducing clothing expenses, eating at cheaper restaurants, and eating out less frequently. You may not be able to drive an expensive car anymore. In fact, you will probably want to sell yours and buy an inexpensive junker that does not involve payments. You may have to fix it, but at least it does not carry monthly payments of $450 or more.

Becoming financially stable may be one of the hardest things you will do. The emotional trauma of cutting the frills and getting back to the basics just when you have really begun to enjoy "the good life" can be frightening. Yet unless you tackle the issue quickly, you may never be in a position to be reconciled, or for that matter to remarry, with any hope of success.

Single Again

Becoming stable again requires building a new life as a mature, single adult. Look yourself in the eye in the mirror and say to yourself, "Hey, I am single. I am willing to be single, and I am going to make it work. I am going to balance my life out." Frankly, you are not ready to be married until you are content to be single, that is, until you get both feet on the ground and establish yourself. Sit back and let that soak in a minute. This is a most important point that I do not want you to overlook.

If you are struggling emotionally, you need to stay out of another relationship. All you do is take that baggage with you, and it can strain the next relationship to the breaking point. Can you imagine the cumulative effect of all those unresolved emotions—those left over from the first relationship added to those of the most recent relationship? You need to regroup and stabilize yourself before you consider another relationship.

While you are endeavoring to accept your single state, you can benefit from many sources of help. Developing (or redeveloping) a personal relationship with Jesus Christ will get you off to the right start. He is the Friend who will never fail. As Charles Spurgeon said, "I have a great need for Christ; I have a great Christ for my needs." The more you learn about Him, the more you will be able to lean on Him in times of uncertainty. Joining a Bible study group, setting aside some quiet time for meditation and prayer, and reading the Word daily are some things you can do to deepen your understanding of Him.

Sometimes counseling is necessary to see you through this

stage. Many good Christian counselors are trained to deal with the problems of the newly single. Your pastor may be able to fill this need or recommend someone who can. In many communities, support groups have been formed to meet on a regular basis and discuss problems and feelings specific to divorced persons. Friends who have always stood by you can be even more important now. Be willing to take advantage of all the support systems available to you.

What About Remarriage?

Part of the process of regaining control is re-evaluating the possibility of another marriage relationship. There are many negatives to remarriage—negatives many people fail to see until after they are married again. Suddenly they can fill pages with reasons why they should *not* have remarried. If only they had listed them twenty-four hours before the ceremony, they could have saved themselves much heartache.

Time is your ally, not your enemy. The more time you can buy, the better your next relationship will be, and the more quality you can build into it.

Time gives you an opportunity to assess how remarriage will affect your children. Initially, they will be overzealous in their attempts to get you to remarry, but they will eventually calm down. In fact, the longer you are single, the more the children will feel secure with the single family unit. They can often shift from being supportive to being resistive once reconciliation begins. This is also true in remarriage, once the wedding date has been set.

In Jim and Bonnie's case, the girls had grown accustomed to having their mother all to themselves. They were the center of her world. Jim's return was greeted with little enthusiasm, since they knew he would absorb a lot of Mom's attention. Nor did they quickly accept his emphasis on neatness, since Mom had been much easier on them.

A Biblical Model

A person who faced a difficult process of reconciliation was Joseph, the biblical hero described in Genesis 37–45. Let's examine how he regained control over his life before he was reconciled to his brothers who had sold him to slave traders. Transplanted from a wealthy land-and-cattle-owner's home into the home of a highly placed military leader, Joseph faced emotional and spiritual alienation. Rather than allow himself to be overwhelmed by self-pity, he set out to do the best job possible in the household of Potiphar.

Remember Bonnie? After the divorce she recalls, "I would go on crying jags. I'd say that I was not worthy of anyone's love." One day her oldest daughter said, "Mom, I don't know why you say that. I love you."

That helped her stop feeling sorry for herself, and she began to take better care of herself. She learned to like herself. In fact, she got to be quite happy with herself. When Jim showed up again and asked that they attempt reconciliation, she was quite a different person from the one he had divorced.

The biblical account reveals how God responded to Joseph's take-charge attitude: "And the LORD was with Joseph, so he became a successful man" (Gen. 39:2). His faithfulness resulted in his gaining control over the household of Potiphar: "[Potiphar] made him overseer over his house, and all that he owned he put in his charge" (Gen. 39:4). If only the brothers who had rejected him could have seen him then! Yet God did not consider Joseph ready for reconciliation with his alienated brothers. Joseph clearly had more to learn before he could gain control of his ego.

The Lord next let Joseph experience the trauma of false

accusation, all the more difficult to accept because it grew out of his sexual self-control. Potiphar's wife liked the young man, who was probably in his early twenties. She "looked with desire at Joseph, and she said, 'Lie with me' " (Gen. 39:7). He rejected her advances, but left his garment in his hurry to flee her embraces. She used this to accuse him of attempting to rape her. Potiphar, understandably upset, had Joseph incarcerated.

In prison Joseph revealed how much he had gained control of himself with the Lord's help: "But the LORD was with Joseph and extended kindness to him, and gave him favor in the sight of the chief jailer. And the chief jailer committed to Joseph's charge all the prisoners who were in the jail; so that whatever was done there, he was responsible for it" (Gen. 39:21-22). The Lord even used him to reveal the dreams of the Pharaoh's cupbearer and baker, which accurately revealed their futures.

Later, when Pharaoh was desperate to find an interpreter of his dreams, the cupbearer remembered Joseph's unique God-given ability. Again God was with Joseph, catapulting him to national leadership under the Pharaoh after he explained to the astonished ruler that his dream meant seven fat years would be followed by seven lean years. Wouldn't this have been a marvelous time for Joseph to send for his brothers and father, inviting them to see him in his new role? Yet reconciliation clearly could not have taken place, for the brothers were not ready for it.

The drought brought the brothers to Egypt. Probably because they came from a foreign land, they had to appear before Joseph, who recognized them immediately even though they did not recognize him. Read how he put them through their paces in an attempt to see if they had changed enough to risk reconciliation (see Gen. 42–44). Only after he sensed a new spirit among them, a new loyalty to the members of the family, did he risk identifying himself to them.

The scene described in Genesis 45 can bring tears to our eyes, for in the reconciliation we see the forgiving heart of a man who could have terrorized his brothers. Joseph first gained emotional control as he saw God's hand in what had happened to him: "And now do not be grieved or angry with yourselves, because you sold me here; for God sent me before you to preserve life" (Gen. 45:5).

In Jim and Bonnie's case reconciliation was not possible until Jim realized he needed God in his life. That freed him to begin the process of working toward reconciliation, but it also made the power of God active in his life.

Joseph also gained financial control of his life. As long as he was a slave in the household of Potiphar, he could not invite the family to join him. Once he became the controller of the resources of Egypt, he could relocate them in the land of Goshen, one of the most pleasant territories in all of Egypt. This attitude is in sharp contrast to Ben, mentioned at the beginning of this chapter, who was willing to let his wife carry the load financially so he could enjoy her presence.

Finally, Joseph kept himself under control during the time he tested his brothers' loyalty to the family. He could easily have identified himself the first time, but he clearly had the leading from the Lord that they were not ready. He was willing to wait until they were ready.

When I counsel couples, I urge them to take time to get reacquainted and determine whether they are ready for another level of relationship. (This is all part of the friendship covenant, which I will explain in more detail later.) They commit themselves to avoiding any sexual activity so that the natural growth of a deeper level of friendship is not short-circuited by sexual satisfaction. Many couples may enjoy each other's company in bed while they cannot stand each other in the kitchen and living room. Sexual compatability does not guarantee successful matrimony.

Though not infallible, the following explanation of the recovery checklist (Fig. 6.2) will indicate whether you have regained a level of personal control over your life. This will reveal areas that need more attention under the guidance of the Holy Spirit through a Christian counselor.

1. *Finances:* Are you able to stand on your own and meet your own needs? This may mean being willing to drop several levels on the socioeconomic ladder and live on less.

2. *Schedule:* Are you getting up on time, getting enough sleep, taking care of yourself, and keeping appointments? Do you complete your projects and tasks by the due date?

3. *Legal:* Are you willing to stop the divorce process and allow reconciliation a chance? This means showing a stance of openness.

4. *Rational:* Are you willing to put aside your anger and bitterness and act like a mature adult? You can't blame the "friend" for everything, because it takes two people.

5. *Spiritual:* Are you a member actively involved in a local church? When your life is unstable, you need the strength and support of others.

6. *In-laws:* Are you willing to be civil and friendly toward your in-laws? You need all the support you and your children can get. They are still your children's grandparents, and friendliness begets friendliness.

7. *Commitment:* Are you stable enough to make a sincere commitment to reconciliation for one year? Many think it's easier to get married, but how stable can that commitment be?

8. *Counsel:* Are you seeking counsel from those over you, according to Hebrews 13:17? This is a time for objective, biblical directives to prevent you from cycling back to a second marriage and possibly a second divorce.

9. *Guidance:* Are you willing to put in the time, effort, and energy to demonstrate that you are open to instruction? The test here is to see if you are willing to learn from your mistakes.

10. *Singleness:* Can you be single and content? It is important that you be able to stand by yourself emotionally before you move on to reconcile or meet someone else.

11. *Friendships:* Are you able to have a good same-sex friend? Lack of close friends will force you to expect too much of anyone in a relationship.

12. *Devotions:* Are you consistent in your time with the Lord in prayer and study of the Word? This time provides all the vitamins for your spiritual and emotional development.

13. *Grace:* Are you open to God's directions to His prophet, Hosea? In order to understand God's grace toward us, we need to extend it to others.

14. *Emotional:* Are you able to control your emotions for short periods of time? The first step is to go one day at a time and then build stability on that.

15. *Guilt:* Are you willing to ask forgiveness for your wrongs in the marriage? If we expect others to do something, we have to lead by example.

Fig. 6.2. Recovery Checklist
Check the appropriate answer to the following statements:

YES NO
1. ___ ___ I am financially able to survive on my own.
2. ___ ___ I am keeping my schedule and responsibilities.
3. ___ ___ I am willing to put all legal proceedings on hold.
4. ___ ___ I am able to be civil to my ex-mate's "friend."
5. ___ ___ I am involved in a spiritual support group.
6. ___ ___ I am friendly to my in-laws.

7. ___ ___ I am committed to at least one year of honest reconciliation.
8. ___ ___ I am willing to seek mature spiritual counsel.
9. ___ ___ I am open to relationship instruction.
10. ___ ___ I am seriously considering remaining single if I cannot reconcile.
11. ___ ___ I am committed to at least one intimate same-sex friend.
12. ___ ___ I am spiritually growing and spending weekly time in the Word.
13. ___ ___ I have finished reading the book of Hosea for the third time.
14. ___ ___ I am able to go at least one week without crying or losing emotional control.
15. ___ ___ I am clean before the Lord by having confessed my sins in my former marriage.

==
___ Total of YES answers

Yes Answers
1-5:   Take more time to heal
6-10:   Consider a friendship agreement
11-15:   Consider relationship instruction or remarriage

Recognizing Differences

Men, remember what it was like to go shopping together? You parked the car and headed for the front door of the department store. Since you held the door for her, she was several steps ahead of you as you started down the aisle. One aisle probably led to women's clothing and another aisle led to the perfume and make-up counter. Your eyes swept to the right for a moment, just long enough for her to disappear to the left to the blouse section.

Like most men, you were mentally unprepared for these detours. As you approached the store, you had again determined that you were going to buy some bath mats, so you were heading for the bath section. Of course, if you shopped often enough with her, you eventually realized she always stopped at the clothing section, the perfume counter, and the purses before she was even mentally ready to consider shopping for anything. Meanwhile you cooled your heels in various awkward positions—or murmured encouragingly as she examined blouses, dresses, and sweaters or sprayed cologne on her wrist. Your father never prepared you for any of this!

Some day you may want to do an informal survey. First, take your position by the entrance next to the women's clothes and count the number of women who stop on one or both sides of the aisle to examine the newest garments on display. Then repeat the observation in the men's section. You will find men typically approach their section purposefully and begin the process of selecting a specific item.

Women, that's why men become so impatient when you are able to get them along on a shopping expedition. They are there for a purpose, and one purpose only—to get the item needed as quickly and as effectively as possible. That is why long ago my wife started leaving me home when she went shopping.

The point I am making is that women approach many things differently from men, and shopping habits are only one minor example. Unless both men and women realize this and actually put this knowledge into their mental computers, the chances of continuing friction are high. In an approach to reconciliation, it is doubly important for men and women to recognize their differences.

Differing Response Cycles

As if that is not a big enough problem in relationship building, we also must recognize that physiologically and emotionally men and women respond differently to what is happening as they spend time together. Remember the graph in Chapter Three on interpersonal relationship development? The man progresses from friendship (social) to physical to emotional to sexual, and the woman progresses from friendship (social) to emotional to physical to sexual. Notice how they flip-flop in the middle?

Many men and women are not aware of this specific difference in response as the relationship develops. As we saw earlier, when the man is ready for the physical contact of kissing, holding hands, and embracing, the woman becomes emotionally involved. She thinks he has made a commitment, while all he is doing is following some friend's advice on how to warm her up for sexual activity.

At this point, she probably begins to respond physically, and her response arouses him emotionally. All she wants is to feel his arms around her and to sense that he loves her by the way he kisses her. On the other hand, he sees her response as readiness for sexual activity. Expectations on both sides are going to be disappointed.

This seesaw response pattern carries over into marriage. Men and women who do not recognize their differences are forever getting their signals crossed. The husband is frustrated because he often misreads his wife's responses and she is disappointed because he doesn't seem to understand her expectations.

Response to Authority

As their hours together accumulate, they also differ in their thought responses to authority. As long as the relationship is at the getting-to-know-each-other stage, neither reads a whole lot into questions about the other's activity. Once there is commitment to each other, the issue of authority surfaces.

Think back to a time five years or so after you were married. Your wife may have developed a specific pattern of activity after getting up in the morning. You discover, for example, that she showers only on days when she washes her hair. One morning you are lying there, thinking about getting up, when she beats you to the bathroom. Since that is rather unusual, you reason she may need to get ready early and she will probably shower. So to determine whether or not to get up promptly, you ask, "Are you going to take a shower this morning?"

That is an innocent question. Right?

Wrong.

"Why? Are you telling me I need to wash my hair?"

Oh, no, she is on the defensive. You have clearly crossed

the border from seeking information to asserting authority over her body. Now how do you extricate yourself?

"Honey, I just was trying to find out if I should leave the shower for you and stay in bed a little longer," you counter in your most reassuring voice.

"You think I don't know when I need to wash my hair?" she retorts.

See what is happening? Somewhere along the line she began to resent what she perceives as your exercise of authority, either because she is unsure about hers or because you stepped beyond the boundary of what she perceives your authority over her should be at that level of your relationship. Yet you perceived it as merely the growing authority people develop over each other as their level of commitment to each other increases. Notice that incorrect *perception* seems to be at the root of these misunderstandings.

Many relationships are sundered because those involved do not understand the differences between men and women. You may be a victim of this. You may have tried to change the way your spouse responded because you did not recognize the basis of that response. You have to adjust to a lot of inherent differences and gain clearer insight into them if you are to be reconciled or remarried.

I find it interesting that most people do not try to "fix" their friends, but they always want to fix the person with whom they have a relationship or to whom they are married. They visualize how they want that person to be and then undertake a fix-it move that says, "Here is a list of all the things *you* need to do to get your life right. Then I will talk to you."

One way to halt this destructive process is to start thinking, *I am willing to give*, instead of, *Here's what I want to take*. That attitude is difficult to cultivate, but it can save your marriage and/or reduce the hostility level in a sundered relationship.

Marriage partners need to visualize what God wants each of them to be and discover how God wants them to behave, rather than demand certain responses from each other. That, too, is part of the acceptance of the differences of the sexes. The most important authority to which we must respond is God's, and a strong prayer life will help us learn how to distinguish the proper actions. We know that we are to "pray without ceasing" (1 Thess. 5:17) and that we are to "pray for one another, so that [we] may be healed" (James 5:16). This healing can apply to relationships as well as to physical illnesses.

Both Need Companionship

Before I list specific differences between men and women, let me emphasize that both men and women need companionship. When God saw Adam at work naming the animals, He saw that Adam did not find a satisfactory relationship with any of them. The biblical record in Genesis reports that God said, "It is not good for the man to be alone; I will make him a helper suitable for him" (2:18). Thus "God fashioned into a woman the rib which He had taken from the man, and brought her to the man" (2:22). Adam recognized what God had done for him: "And the man said, 'This is now bone of my bones,/And flesh of my flesh;/She shall be called Woman,/Because she was taken out of Man' " (2:23). The intensity of the companionship is then described, "For this cause a man shall leave his father and his mother, and shall cleave to his wife; and they shall become one flesh" (2:24).

I find it significant that this companionship grew out of their relationship to God. Before Eve appeared on the scene, Adam had a consistent pattern of communication with God, based on a clearly vital relationship with his Creator. Then God created Eve in a very personal way. Both Adam and Eve recognized the sound of the Lord God walking in the garden after their transgression, so they clearly had a regular level of communication with Him after Eve's creation.

Thus, both men and women need vital, personal communication with God through prayer, to equip them to communicate with each other at a significant level. This companionship with God can significantly strengthen a marriage where there are a lot of differences. A wise man once said, "Successful marriage is always a triangle: a man, a woman, and God."

Jim and Bonnie, you will remember, had been married fourteen years when they were divorced. Bonnie loved God and had a personal relationship with Jesus Christ. Jim was a churchgoer, but he had never made the personal commitment that put him under the authority of God. As a result, when Bonnie sought a warm, loving relationship like the one she had experienced with her first husband, who was also a vital Christian, she discovered (too late) that Jim could not provide it.

Five years after their divorce, Jim turned his life over to Jesus Christ. Immediately he recognized his need to restore the relationship with Bonnie. He believed God would help them work things out. Because of that commitment, he and Bonnie both kept going despite frustrating months of no apparent progress. Once they embarked on a program of close interaction under the guidance of a counselor, they discovered that they could really like each other. (Later in this book, I will describe this program for you in more detail.) As their sense of companionship grew, they realized they were truly in love with each other. Companionship with God helped them find the human companionship they were looking for in each other.

Differences between Men and Women

Many of the differences mentioned in the following pages are culturally conditioned. Yet they are just as real as if we were born with them. These characteristics seem to become more distinct when a relationship breaks down and the gap between husband and wife widens. We will look at them in terms of reconciliation, and all the applications will be to the reconciliation process. A similar description may be found in *Just Me and the Kids* by Patricia Brandt and David Jackson.

I want to emphasize that this is not a sexual identity test. If you find yourself on any particular side, you must remember that we are looking at these characterizations only to identify *general* differences between men and women. Do not regard them as absolutes.

Suppose that you are a woman who has grown up with several brothers. You may do many things as men do them. Or if you are a man who had many sisters and little male influence, you may react in many ways as they react. Such situations reinforce my statement that I am only providing general guidelines on how to view the reactions of the opposite sex.

Overall Cultural Differences

Men tend to be providers. They teach and give direction. As they develop their strengths in these areas, they use them to develop their manhood and their self-esteem.

Women are basically protective and womb centered. They want to guard, conserve, and nourish.

What happens in the breakup of a home in which a man and a woman have been developing these characteristics? Both areas go to pieces. The man is no longer able to provide, and the woman is no longer able to protect. In his drive to provide, the man will go to one of two extremes: (1)

He will provide everything, move out and sleep in a camper, and send the whole paycheck home every week; or (2) he will provide nothing, take everything within sight, and leave. If he can provide, he will often overprovide and overcompensate. If he cannot provide it all, he will not provide anything.

The woman, on the other hand, will do her best to protect the home, even if it means locking him out and never letting him in again. He has a shirt, a pair of pants, and a pair of shoes, and that is enough, in her opinion. He can call or knock persistently, but she will refuse him entry because she is trying to protect her home.

Specific Differences

Beyond these broad cultural differences, a man and a woman differ in many specific ways. For example, when a man buys his wife an electric drill for an anniversary present, he is pleased with himself for acting appropriately in buying her a gift—without being reminded of the upcoming occasion. He tends to be logical, and he is oriented toward the practical side of life. But his wife is much more emotional, and her thoughts often dwell on love and romance. His self-satisfaction will be short-lived when he discovers his wife was expecting a diamond ring. Her reaction to the present of the drill will not be at all what he expected. Yet if they have been married for any time at all—or if they really know much about each other—they should know how each differs from the other. She should appreciate the fact that he has done his best in his choice of a gift, and he should remember to send a small bouquet of flowers to her.

This example may seem to deal with relatively minor differences compared to those that may have confronted some of you in your marriage. But these differences do mount up and, added to the weight of the major differences, can overburden many relationships to their breaking points.

Let's look at some of the differences to keep in mind during the reconciliation process.

Objective versus subjective. A man will normally sit down as he faces a situation or problem, list things, step back, examine all the angles, and then draw factual conclusions as he describes the problem. He looks for facts.

A woman is generally very subjective. She takes everything personally and feels that the whole problem is her fault—*she* messed up her marriage. She looks for feelings.

Now these two try to reconcile with each other. From her subjective position, the wife wants to resolve her hurt first. From his objective position the husband wants to solve the living situation and to discuss finances and their property. She decides he is after money and is going to get all he can; she thinks he does not care about her need and her hurt. The only way she knows to get even is to get at his money and possessions. I have watched as a woman went into the garage, gathered up all her husband's tools, and then threw them into the rain. For her, that was a "logical" reaction, but he failed to see any logic in it at all.

Logical versus intuitive. He approaches the divorce as though he is working out the details of a construction contract. When he presents a list and says, "You get this...I get that...let's sit down and work it out," she is so upset she cannot see the page. He wants her to cooperate, but she does not care. Nothing matters, nothing is going to be right again—it will be all or nothing. The attorney for each determines they need to go for all they can get, so the list each partner carries to the meeting has 100 per cent of all the property. Nothing gets resolved.

Impersonal versus personal. He can stand back and take all the facts into consideration, while she takes everything he does in a reconciling situation personally. He promises to be at an appointment by 7:00, but he calls at 7:17 to say he is out of gas on a country road. By then she is an emotional wreck and doesn't even hear what he is saying. By the time he puts the phone down, his ear is so hot he can almost feel smoke coming from it. The fact that he was two miles from the nearest telephone and ran all the way in the rain makes no difference to her. He is late!

Neglectful versus nagging. Husbands tend to be neglectful, especially when they are under pressure. When that happens, wives begin to nag. Then the more she nags, the more neglectful he becomes. Now that they are separated and trying to be reconciled, the wife goes on and on and on, relentlessly. She wants this done or that done, and she wants to know why he hasn't taken care of something else.

He feels as though he hears the same tape recording every time he shows up. The more times he hears this tape, the less he really hears of what is on it. In fact, the more she repeats it, the less chance there is of his doing what she wants done.

The devastating truth is that he is discouraged because he cannot be a provider, he cannot be objective, and he cannot really do all those things she wants because he cannot get into the house. And she is lonely because no man is in the house, and if he would only "straighten up," she would let him in the house and she wouldn't be lonely anymore. They are caught up in a cycle of their own doing, and it is undoing them both.

Practical versus aesthetic. Men tend toward the practical, women toward the aesthetic. When a couple separates, he says very practically, "We cannot afford to keep up two households. We need to sell the house so we both can live with the divided income." She looks at him and says, "I'd rather live in a tent. I am going to stay in this house—no matter what."

Three months later he is unable to keep up the payments, and in nine months the house is repossessed. All the equity is lost to the finance company. Both partners say they don't care, and some real estate firm emerges as the winner of this emotional situation.

Present minded versus future minded. Men are forever looking ahead, while women tend to be concerned about the present. Men have a tendency to be the first to talk about reconciliation, but women are still so wound up emotionally that the mere mention of reconciliation is like throwing gasoline on a fire.

A man will come by with his girlfriend in his car to pick up the kids and say, "In a couple of weeks we ought to sit down and talk about getting back together again," as he waltzes out of the house. This is not the time or place to talk about reconciliation.

Initiator versus responder. Very often the conflict that led to separation results in the natural relationships being turned around. Where he once led, she now begins to demand or push. He gets tired of it and says, "Do whatever you want. I am tired of the emotional hassle." He cannot handle the emotional pressure, but she is not really ready to lead. She has to make decision after decision at a time when she is in no shape to make even one. Eventually the husband says, "Sell the house and the car. Keep the kids."

The newspapers reported that a man saw an ad: "Like new Porsche Targa for sale. $500." He went by to look at it and couldn't believe the price. "You mean $5,000, don't you?" he asked.

"No," the woman answered, "$500."

He took the car for a spin, and when he returned, he was still incredulous.

"You've got to be kidding," he told the woman.

She wasn't, so he took out his checkbook and wrote a check for $500. After he gave her the check he asked, "Tell me, why would you sell it for $500?"

She said, "Simple. My husband ran off with his secretary

to Mexico and wrote that I should sell the car and send him the money. So I'll send him the money!"

Consistent versus adaptable. Under emotional stress women have a tendency to be adaptable. They are so caught up with trying to adapt themselves to the situation that they do not have any time to take care of details. They do not have time to pay the bills, balance the checkbook, clean the house, or take care of themselves.

Men, on the other hand, are consistent in their irritability. They have a tendency to come around and harass the life out of the women they left. They will not be polite enough to send the child support by mail. Instead, they bring it in person, send it special delivery by a girlfriend, or even have the girlfriend write out the check.

Straightforward versus sensitive. The men are the straightforward ones and the women the sensitive ones. For example, in trying for reconciliation women approach it heart first. They are highly vulnerable to misinterpreted information. They tend to overreact because they want to be reconciled so badly.

The men, on the other hand, have a tendency to be too cut-and-dried. A man may say, "Okay, we are going to get a divorce, or we are not going to get a divorce. You have to tell me by November 15 because I want to know which it is." She says, "But that's our anniversary." He hadn't even thought of that—it was just another date to him.

Soul modest—body free versus body modest—soul free. He is willing to undress physically, but he will not reveal his soul to her. She needs and wants to undress emotionally but to stay dressed physically. Neither wants to meet on the other's turf. He does not understand why another woman, a separation, or even a divorce should interfere with their sexual relationship, and she feels like a prostitute who doesn't get paid. What she really needs is his focused attention, a strong hug, and two to three hours of soul talk.

When two persons who have been married for a long time engage in conflict so severe that they separate, they have a tendency to bounce away from each other. But sooner or later they gravitate back to each other because of the relational and sexual forces in their lives (remember the effects of homeostasis). Often they will oscillate back and forth—driven apart emotionally but brought together physically. They approach each other for different reasons—she for emotional support, he for physical assurance—but both arrive at the same place, in bed together.

The most harmful thing you can do during an attempt at reconciliation is to stir in the physical element. To achieve genuine reconciliation you need to reconcile emotionally first and take some positive relational steps before going too quickly into the physical.

There are two extremes. Her response usually is, "Keep your hands off me until we are completely, 100 per cent united. Then I'll consider it." His response tends to be, "If I cannot have a little physical contact along the way, forget it. I don't want any part of it." In essence both are saying, "You meet my needs, and *then* I'll meet yours." As long as they insist on this tradeoff, they both lose. When there are two demanders and no givers, the environment for reconciliation is destroyed.

On the other hand, some couples say, "The physical is all we want now. We'll take care of the emotional later." This approach only creates a backwash of unresolved problems. The relationship may seem to progress, but its uncertain base will eventually give way.

Balance is desperately needed. He needs to provide emotional commitment in that he stops seeing other women. She needs to provide a physical response even if she does not feel like it at first. It is important that the two work out this balance to meet their mutual needs.

Perhaps I should stress those words: *the two work out this balance.* They cannot just passively hope for it to occur. They must be willing to strive toward that goal. The fruit of the Holy Spirit, especially patience and self-control (see Gal. 5:22–23), can bolster their resolve in this. A certain amount of cooperation will be required too. Rely upon the Lord's guidance and counsel in this matter as in all others and earnestly ask to know His will, for He has said, "I will instruct you and teach you in the way which you should go;/I will counsel you with My eye upon you" (Ps. 32:8).

If they are finally divorced, the physical relationship must wait until remarriage. I know of a woman who continued sleeping with her husband even after their divorce was final. She became pregnant, and their lives got rather complicated, especially since they were seeing other people. Sin has many consequences.

Aggressive versus submissive. Men are naturally aggressive and women are naturally submissive. During conflict they may reverse roles. He will yell at her; she will cry and then throw things. He submits to it and leaves. This may be repeated over and over again, with neither of them keeping their natural roles. Since neither will try to resolve the problem, they blow apart. Only as one reverts to the more natural role can the cycle be broken.

Egotistical versus jealous. A man's basic problem, as women see it, is his tremendous ego. His head is two sizes too large for his body, but he doesn't realize it because he is so pleased with himself.

The first thing a woman attacks when she is responding emotionally is his ego. She knows where he is all stitched up, and she knows how to cut his stitches loose. She does her best to deflate his confidence in himself.

His immediate response to such an attack is probably along the lines of naming the other women in his life who are sewing him back up again. He tries to make her jealous, but he also makes the point that there are other people who are positive forces in his life while she is so negative. Of course, he may do or say other things just to generate jealousy so that he can set her off, even though she may have a legitimate reason for her initial strong reaction.

These differences can be charted by using Figure 7.1, developed by Susan Smith. Each of you estimate your percentage of identity with each set of opposing traits. Then compare your scores and see what areas need better understanding.

The Move toward Reconciliation

To reconcile, two things have to happen. First, you have to change roles.

Women, you need to build up the man's ego if you are trying to be reconciled. You have to compliment him, encourage him, and feed him positive input. If you do not do it, someone else will gravitate in his direction.

I know women who truly want to be reconciled, yet they are doing all the wrong things. Whenever the man comes around, she unloads on him, and she never stops the entire time he is around her. By contrast, a sweet young thing in the office will get his coffee, polish his desk, and arrange his appointments. Where do you think he will go?

On the other hand, I meet men who are trying to achieve reconciliation while they are dating actively. They cannot understand why their wives get upset over this. Men, you must understand what that does in the life of a woman.

So let me repeat: If you want to achieve reconciliation, you will have to change roles. If you are normally physical and she is emotional, you now will have to be emotional and she physical. Both call for an act of the will. Be assured that the Holy Spirit gives us both the will to obey and the power to do it (see Rom. 15:13; 2 Tim. 1:7).

Fig. 7.1. Relational Differences

(Relational differences are determined by heredity, gender, experience, and cultures, but they must be dealt with effectively in order to facilitate any relational development.)

INSTRUCTIONS: Estimate the per cent of time you demonstrate the following characteristics (the total should equal 100 per cent).

EXAMPLE:

Willing to take risks	80 | 20	Cautious

1.	Objective	____|____	Subjective
2.	Logical	____|____	Intuitive
3.	Impersonal	____|____	Personal
4.	Tends to neglect	____|____	Tends to complain
5.	Practical	____|____	Aesthetic
6.	Future minded	____|____	Present minded
7.	Initiator	____|____	Responder
8.	Consistent	____|____	Adaptable
9.	Communication is to the point	____|____	Communication is sensitive to others
10.	Soul modest, body free	____|____	Soul free, body modest
11.	Aggressive	____|____	Submissive
12.	Egotistical	____|____	Jealous
13.	Needs a sense of significance	____|____	Needs a sense of security
14.	Task oriented	____|____	People oriented
15.	Physical	____|____	Emotional
16.	Passionate	____|____	Romantic
17.	Defeated by discouragement	____|____	Defeated by loneliness

Developed in conjunction with Susan Smith, 1985.

Second, you have to recognize the role of significance and security. The man wants significance, and the woman wants security. In reconciliation, it is important that the woman makes her husband feel significant and that he makes her feel secure. He cannot expect her to respond well if he will not pay his child support and provide additional financial security. I know that, legally, child visitation is a right without child support. Yet just because it is legal does not mean she can accept it emotionally.

In addition, just as a man must be able to support his family financially, he must be able to support them emotionally. Ralph, for example, told me that he has tried to reconcile for four years, but he has given up and is getting married in three months. When I asked him how long he has been going with his future wife, he said, "Three years." From where I sit, that is not providing emotional security or seeking reconciliation—that is two-timing it!

A woman needs to learn to focus on the man's positives and build his ego. That is the opposite of the natural response, but that is what is vitally needed. Even if he has married someone else, this should still occur, especially in front of the children so that they do not grow to hate their father. If they already hate him, the mother has taught them to hate a parent and some day they may well hate her.

Statistics show that the better the relationship between the parents, the more consistent the child support and the larger the size of the payment, as well as the help above what is legally required. So the financial reason alone may be enough for you to consider reconciliation. Remember, the goal is not remarriage, but a friendly, harmonious relationship.

Facing Reality

What is the most difficult experience for the person involved in separation or divorce? Each of you has your own truly difficult experience, which may be leaving the children or establishing independence. Yet let me suggest that throughout separation and the early years of divorce, the most difficult thing you will ever do is face reality.

Everyone going through a tough experience like divorce tends to live in a fantasy world. One such fantasy is that separation and divorce will bring peace. You may find temporary periods of peace, but unless you make some major adjustments you will continue to experience significant conflict.

How do you begin to face reality? First, you need to face the reality of what has happened emotionally. Do not try to make things different from what they are. Accept your situation, and begin a plan of action to move toward the next step in your life.

I find that many people want instant solutions to everything. They want to stop hurting; they want things to be right, nice, peaceful, and secure—_now_. In reality, emotionally it will probably not be that way for quite a while.

During this period of emotional upheaval, you need to take the time to develop a plan of action. Write down the steps you think you need to take, share them with a noninvolved person, and seek counsel. The support of a person whose judgment you trust will do a lot to steer you in the right direction.

Remember our discussion of the alienation that takes place right after separation? Normally, people are so disoriented, angry, frustrated, and unhappy that they do not act rationally for quite some time. To help you inject sanity into how you react and what you do, you must get with someone who will be honest with you. You do not need a cover-up; you need reality.

Four Key Questions

Here are four questions to help you determine where you are: (1) What are you the day *before* you get married: married or single? (2) What are you the day *after* you get married: married or single? (3) What are you the day *before* you have your final decree? (4) What are you the day *after* you have your final decree?

Why do I ask such simple questions? Frankly, I see people separating, building new relationships, proposing, and setting wedding dates while they are still waiting for their final decree. A couple came in recently, for example, and wanted to talk about getting married.

"Are you free to get married?" I asked.

"Well, I think so," the man replied. "My wife filed for a divorce, as far as I know."

The woman looked at her fiancé and said, "I didn't know you were married before."

Not responding directly to her, he said, "Well, it is just a minor legal technicality I have to take care of." That "minor technicality" had her whole life in jeopardy, something she clearly did not appreciate.

Reality says that if you do not have a final decree in hand, you are still a married person and you are to act like one. Even if you only need to send thirty dollars to the attorney, do one of two things: (1) Take care of it and then start dating; or (2) act like a married person until you have the final decree. I know no one wants to hear this, but for your own sanity and for the health of any relationship you want to enter into, act in keeping with the reality of your marital status.

You Are Responsible

Another aspect of emotional reality is that circumstances are no more responsible for your attitude and actions than a mirror is for the way you look. *You* are responsible for them. If you are a Christian, the other person can never wrong you so much to justify your becoming cruel, spiteful, and unfriendly. All these circumstances reveal is the real you—the kind of person you really are inside.

One woman came to me with forty-three pages of what her husband had done wrong. I have counseled many people who have filled notebooks with thirty to thirty-five pages of single-spaced wrongs inflicted by a spouse. The most important counsel I give them is to *burn the book.*

"But he'll never deal with the things if I don't tell him about them," she insists.

My question is, "Will he deal with them if you present them?"

A friend's secretary had an alcoholic, abusive husband. As Christians, my friend and the secretary united in prayer for the man, but he only became more abusive. Eventually the couple started talking about divorce, though neither really wanted it. One day the secretary arrived at the office in unusually good spirits.

"Last night my husband and I talked for two hours. All

the walls came down. Not once did we start arguing," she revealed.

Over a period of ten days she reported that their relationship was getting better and better. In fact, her husband's drinking had declined to two cans of beer an evening, compared to his usual eight or ten per evening. What had made the difference?

"The evening before the breakthrough in communication I was praying for my husband and became really desperate. Instead of asking God to change my husband I told Him, 'Lord, change me. I cannot change my husband, so I hand him over to You.' As soon as I did that, peace filled my heart, and I got the assurance that my husband would change dramatically, overnight," she confessed later.

"The next evening I told him, 'I'm not going to try to change you. I'm going to let the Lord do that.' The moment I said that I could see him sit up, as though a big load had been lifted off his back. I continued, 'I really respect you for the hard work you do. You're an intelligent man; and I respect you for your accomplishments.' As I said this he was looking down at his hands. When I finished, he looked up with tears in his eyes and said, 'I really appreciate that.'"

As a result of that two-hour, very personal communication, this secretary's husband began treating her "like he used to treat me when we were dating." Their sex life, interrupted for nearly a year, became normal again.

What thirty-page list of wrongs could have brought on that change? How much counseling would have done it (even if he had been willing to go for counseling, which he wasn't)? A simple prayer on the part of the believing wife, "Lord, change me," brought on a truly unbelievable transformation in an unbelieving, abusive, alcoholic husband. Remember, change starts with *you*.

Focus on what you can do, and don't worry about what you cannot do. The apostle Paul's admonition in Philippians 4:6–7 applies even in your situation: "Be anxious for nothing, but in everything by prayer and supplication with thanksgiving let your requests be made known to God. And the peace of God, which surpasses all comprehension, shall guard your hearts and your minds in Christ Jesus."

Developing emotional stability based on the reality of your situation will equip you to begin to stand alone. Learn not to depend emotionally upon somebody else. Many people get married to have someone to lean on, and when divorce occurs, they immediately look for someone else to lean on. It takes four feet on the ground to make a marriage work—not two one-legged people looking for someone to hold them up.

Stand on your own two feet; begin to set your personal, emotional, spiritual, and physical priorities; and strive to accomplish them. Become a giver, not a taker. A taker is someone dashing about with an emotional umbilical cord in hand, looking for someone to plug into, while a giver is someone looking to help another person.

Establish Spiritual Goals

During the trauma leading to divorce and during the initial period afterward, many people neglect spiritual priorities. To develop stability, you need to commit the direction of your life to God. If you are unsure about your relationship with God, confess your sin to Him, asking Jesus Christ to come into your life. God will forgive your sin, send the Holy Spirit to represent Jesus Christ in your life, and give you the power to begin taking the positive steps I have described. In Acts 2:38, we have this assurance: "Repent, and let each of you be baptized in the name of Jesus Christ for the forgiveness of your sins; and you shall receive the gift of the Holy Spirit."

You see, you can hook your life together with another person physically and mentally, but that will not last. We are all spiritual beings, and we need to hook our lives together *spiritually* if our relationships are to last. This is especially true for you if you are trying to be reconciled to your ex, for it takes strength and support far beyond your abilities.

Set a time for consistent Bible study, beginning with the gospel of John if you are a fairly new Christian. Have a daily time of prayer and a weekly fellowship with other believers. Changing yourself and your feelings is a supernatural task and takes a lot more than saying, "I wish I wouldn't feel this way anymore," or "I wish I hadn't said that." The support of fellow believers is vitally important, even if you think you cannot possibly face them in your present condition. Jesus promised: "For where two or three have gathered together in My name, there I am in their midst" (Matt. 18:20).

Begin Meeting People

We all tend to be self-conscious after a traumatic upheaval in our lives. Yet one of the most important things you can do is to force yourself to get out and meet new people. The more you dislike it, the more you need to do it. Initially people may not know exactly how to handle your new status. In time, though, you will begin to feel comfortable with each other.

In the next chapter I will focus on how to be a friend. You will notice that each step calls for effort on your part, but let me remind you that as Christians we are not alone—we have the Holy Spirit to help us.

What About Dating?

The first thing many people want to do after breaking up with a spouse is to start dating again. The solution to a bad relationship is to get into another one as quickly as possible—they think. You may feel the same way about it. Yet you need to ask yourself some questions before jumping onto the dating bandwagon. Give careful consideration to each one before you answer.

1. Am I Free to Date?

I touched on this subject earlier in the chapter, but I want to add a new dimension to this question by analyzing what the Bible teaches about who is free to remarry after a marriage has been sundered by divorce. I offer five typical situations in an attempt to shed some light on this controversial subject.

Situation 1. Believer 1 marries Believer 2. Then Believer 2 commits fornication (see 1 Cor. 5:9–11). Believer 2 confesses the sin (see 1 John 1:9; Pss. 32; 38:18; 51) and no longer is guilty of that sin. Although restoration has priority, divorce by Believer 1 is permitted. There are no grounds for divorce by Believer 2 because Believer 1 has not committed adultery. If divorce occurs, Believer 1 may remarry (see Matt. 19:9). Believer 2 has two choices: (1) Reconcile to Believer 1, if this person has not remarried; or (2) stay single, which obviously affects dating habits.

If both commit adultery and get a divorce, neither may remarry. If they do not reconcile to each other and they marry others, both are committing fornication despite the vows of marriage they may make.

If after a divorce, Believer 2 marries Believer 3, and Believer 3 then commits adultery, Believer 2 may seek divorce. Believer 1 may still be single but cannot now remarry Believer 2 (see Deut. 24:4).

Situation 2. Believer marries Nonbeliever. This marriage is not in agreement with God's principle of believer marrying believer. They may remain married so that the Believer can continue to be a testimony for God in the community (see 1 Cor. 7:14). Believer may divorce Nonbeliever only if the latter commits fornication or leaves (see 1 Cor. 7:15). If that should happen, the first priority is reconciliation on the part of the Believer.

The biblical standards for divorce and remarriage do not apply to the Nonbeliever. If the Nonbeliever leaves or commits adultery and gets a divorce for either reason, the Believer has the right to marry but only to a believer (see 2 Cor. 6:14).

Situation 3. Believer 1 marries Believer 2. If there is no fornication, divorce is not permitted by Scripture. Should separation occur, the goal ought to be reconciliation. If there is a divorce and either remarries, that person is guilty of adultery.

Situation 4. Nonbeliever 1 marries Nonbeliever 2. There is no agreement before God in this marriage, and God has put forth no law in this case. Both are responsible to the moral law of the land (see Rom. 2:14) and to their own conscience (see Rom. 2:15). Though there is no proscription against divorce even without fornication, they should attempt reconciliation first.

Situation 5. Nonbeliever 1 marries Nonbeliever 2. Nonbeliever 1 becomes a believer. The New Believer should remain married and continue to be a testimony for God in the community (see 1 Cor. 7:14) unless Nonbeliever 2 commits fornication or leaves (see 1 Cor. 7:15). Then the first priority for the New Believer is reconciliation with Nonbeliever 2. If Nonbeliever 2 seeks a divorce after committing fornication, the New Believer is free to marry, but only to another believer (see 2 Cor. 6:14).

111

2. Am I Emotionally Free to Date?

Have you recovered enough from the emotional trauma of the divorce to be able to consider a new relationship, or are you simply bouncing off that relationship into another one without any healing? The grieving process after a divorce is often more severe and prolonged than after the death of a mate.

3. Have I Stabilized My Life?

Have you got both feet on the ground, or are you still hobbling around? Have you moved from being a taker to being a giver? Are your finances in order, and is your spiritual life revitalized?

4. Are My Children Ready?

Don't rush into finding a new parent for your children. In a few years, your children will be gone. If you begin dating to find them a parent—and marry one—your marriage may be in trouble after the children are gone. On the other side of that coin, if you marry someone who cannot stand your children, you are also in trouble.

5. Am I Just Looking for Companionship?

Every singles group has a substantial number who say, "I am just coming out of this hurting relationship and am hurting so much. I need somebody to talk to." Companionship is a by-product of the dating process—it should not be the primary purpose for dating. Same-sex friends meet this need most effectively.

6. Can I Afford to Date?

This question is for both men and women. If there are children, the cost of baby-sitters may be a significant factor. If your date has children, you may want to contribute to that cost. So unless you are in a position to cover all the costs of dating, which can mount up to a sizable sum, use discretion.

7. Am I Willing to Be Hurt Again?

Can you handle another broken relationship at this time? People are going to hurt you emotionally at various times over the course of your life, but there is no need to intensify the hurt by dating. The closer people are to you, the more they are going to hurt you.

8. What Do My Parents or Family Think?

What does your support system, your family and friends, really think about your dating again? I have told many women that before they marry again, they ought to seek their father's approval. If you had followed your father's advice the first time, would you have married? If the answer is no, you know where to turn the second time around.

9. Do I Have Clear Moral Standards?

Many adults behave in ways that clearly go against God's laws. A friend of mine lives in a cul-de-sac with six families. Four of the couples separated in a thirty-day period. I don't know about his neighborhood, but I know what has happened in other neighborhoods. Many separated people begin new relationships, even though none of them has a final decree. They are following no moral standard, and they and their children will suffer in the end. The rules you live by must be in accordance with those God has set forth. When you jump out of a ten-story building, it is not falling the ten stories that hurts; it is the sudden stop at the bottom. The same is true when you transgress God's moral law.

10. Will My Dating Affect Reconciliation?

We have discussed this earlier in the example of your ex coming back in a reconciliation move just when you are in the middle of an exciting new relationship. At this point you may prefer the new relationship, but you also know God wants you to be reconciled. Dating may be dangerous to reconciliation—even to reaching the friendship state, much less to preparing for remarriage.

11. Am I Emotionally Ready for Another Divorce?

Dating is often the prelude to marriage. Can you really handle the possibility of another divorce? The risk of divorce in a second marriage is incredibly high. There are more devastating experiences than loneliness, and divorce is one of them.

When you get a divorce, it is like someone reaching down into you and turning you inside out—and then sprinkling salt all over you. Add the experience of alienation for a second time and the prospect of dealing with stepchildren. Imagine dating a mother who does not believe in disciplining her children. You eventually get married. Her child continues to misbehave, and you smack him lightly on the bottom. Can you imagine her reaction? She might even charge you with child abuse. The real rub comes when your child is being disciplined—and you are not the one doing it.

12. Will I Be Able to Meet All My Financial Obligations?

Can you afford to live on what he has left over after making two child support payments each month and paying his other bills? Approximately $2 billion are being paid each year in child support. Unfortunately many couples get married depending on child support to balance the budget, even though less than 30 per cent of all child support is paid. Most men cannot support three families—yours may be the one your ex lets go.

13. Have I Faced the Possibility of Child Abuse?

The incidence of child abuse, which is a serious problem

in blood families, is much higher still in stepfamilies. A person who is disposed to abusing children feels much less constraint when the child is not his or hers biologically. And please do not make the mistake of assuming that only non-Christians abuse children. I assure you it is happening in many Christian families.

14. How Important Is My Church?

Most people get divorced over three things: money, children, and religion. Before you marry, you may agree, "I'll go to my church and you go to yours." But it may not work out that way after the marriage ceremony. The pressures of family and friends easily outweigh promises made during a dating relationship. This should be a serious consideration before you even begin dating.

15. What Is The Age Difference?

Most of us have enough sense to tell our children about the five-year speed limit, that is, they should not date anyone five years older or younger than they are. It is hard to tell yourself that, but it's a fact that a ten-year age difference puts the two of you into totally different decades culturally.

When you are fifty and your spouse is forty, there is a world of difference. Often after fifty a primary preoccupation is with maintaining health and the status quo, but at forty you are still skiing or running up and down mountains. You may also be entering your most productive years.

16. Am I Ready for More Children?

Guess what happens if you are still in the childbearing years? No matter that you both brought children into the marriage. Many times the youngest child will be eight to twelve years younger than the others, and that can really tie you down just when other couples your age are starting to travel and to enjoy the freedom of an empty nest.

17. Am I Prepared for a Fight Over Inheritances?

"Hold it," you say. "I love my spouse and we'll work things out." Yes, but his family or yours might not be willing to do that. Remember, your children bring at least another family into the picture—and if he has children, that adds another.

If you have never been married before, here are some things to remember. Do not move into your partner's house with your furniture. You are better off to sell both houses, get rid of all the furniture, and start from scratch together. This takes about a year to figure out, but it is worth the effort. Too many disputes can begin over things accumulated from the time before your marriage.

I tried to help one couple ahead of time. They refused to follow my advice—after all, they were in their late fifties. She had lived in town all her life, and he had lived on a ranch. When they married, the city woman moved in to his home, where he had kept everything as it was following his first wife's death.

What was it like to be married to a man who was involved in a lot of activities on a big ranch? She was alone often because he had to be out supervising operations on the ranch. Add to that the fact that she was living with the first wife's furniture and belongings, right down to the kitchen utensils. It is no wonder that after a year they decided to sell the ranch and move to town.

Reality is tough to handle at any time, but it is especially hard when you are experiencing alienation and the trauma of divorce. Give yourself time to stabilize. As you pray and seek God's guidance, He can help you deal with your true situation.

Becoming a Friend

What happens when a married couple stay at the acquaintance level and never become friends? Let Jim and Bonnie tell what happened in their marriage.

"After fourteen years of marriage, there was a definite lack of fulfillment in our marriage. There just didn't seem to be a future and continuing on did not seem worth the effort. I had never had feelings of love for Bonnie, but had seen myself as the knight in shining armor that rescued a woman in distress. Now I wanted out," Jim says.

Bonnie states, "We were not communicating from day one. I hated conflict, so I desperately tried to keep from getting into arguments with Jim. I got myself deeply involved at church, where I got a real sense of fulfillment. When Jim left, I devoted myself to the children and the work at church."

Because Jim and Bonnie did not achieve a friendship level at home, a substitute surfaced at school. Jim developed a relationship with another woman that showed him what friendship could be like. To escape what seemed like a marriage going nowhere, he got a divorce, only to discover that none of the new relationships he developed were satisfying either.

What was Jim's problem? He had never really learned what it takes to be a friend. Only when he and Bonnie were willing to follow my advice and commit themselves to spending quality time together were they able to become friends. Basic, of course, was their commitment to God to make the effort to be reconciled at the friendship level.

What is friendship? I describe it as "deep and enduring affection built on mutual respect and esteem." Jim and Bonnie lacked these feelings from the start of their marriage. Jim says, "I felt she let me run over her. I wanted her to be more gutsy. I also thought she spent too much time outside the home."

After the divorce, however, once they spent thirty or more hours a month together, he says, "I started seeing her as a different person. She was more spunky, she liked herself, she was physically more appealing. As a result, I developed new feelings for her."

What made the difference? As a single, Bonnie stabilized her life, developed a new sense of significance, went on a diet, and learned to be more aggressive as a person. She was worth spending time with, even though Jim had asked for her time out of a commitment to God's plan for marriage.

Bill Gothard in Basic Youth Conflicts portrays the four levels of friendship as follows:

1. The *acquaintance level* is fed by occasional contact. You have the freedom to ask general questions such as, "What is your name?" and "Where do you work?" I call these "public information questions," the kind you could find in a phone book. Unfortunately, many marriages operate at that level, exchanging information about work-related events and the children at the end of the day before the husband retires to the television set and the wife tackles her household chores.

2. The *casual level* involves regular contact and shared common interest. You may work together, see each other in the same club, or meet at church in the singles class. You have the freedom to ask specific questions: "I missed you

last week, were you ill?" or "I see you are driving a new car. Did you just buy it?" These questions mean you have had some prior involvement and can ask for more specific information.

3. The *close friendship* level involves planned contact, set appointments, a regular time to get together, the freedom to suggest mutual projects, and the willingness to work together on something that each one of you is working on. For example, you would not ask an acquaintance to come over and work on your car, but you would do it with a close friend. Finally, at this level you begin to see the potential achievement in each other's life. You have the commitment and the bond of responsibility to work on it.

4. The *intimate level* occurs when there is an open honesty, a mutual commitment to each other, and the freedom to confront each other about areas needing improvement. You have the freedom to say to each other, "You should not have done that; it was not right," and still be friends. (We still do not know enough about this level to fully understand it.)

Some people have never recognized what these differences in levels mean. They will approach someone, say, "How are you today?" as a get-acquainted question, and then tell intimate details about the innermost part of their lives. If you are caught in this situation, you may think, *Wait a minute. Hold on. I'm not ready for this yet.* So you excuse yourself to get a cup of coffee.

Friendship is a balance. You need to go down the steps at the same pace, moving through each stage together. Until you can handle that with both men and women, you are really not ready for a relationship-level involvement with another person.

If you need a lot of help in developing friendships, I recommend you get one or more of the following books: *Too Close, Too Soon,* which Bobbie Reed and I wrote together;

Quality Friendship, by Gary Inrig (probably the best book on friendship); and *Friends and Friendship*, by Jerry White.

Yet reading books on friendship cannot replace being a friendly person. You need to start with people who are strangers so that you can develop skills to become friendly with the person with whom you want to be reconciled. Being friendly with strangers is clearly a lot easier than becoming friendly with someone who has hurt you or whom you have hurt deeply.

Unfriendliness Is Contagious

Very few people today remain in the same town for their entire lifetimes. We are a mobile society. As a result, families tend to turn in on themselves, drawing strength from each other instead of from close relatives and neighbors. This not only puts unusual strain on the nuclear family, adding to the pressures that bring about family disintegration, but it also prevents us from developing a wider circle of friends that prepares us for marriage.

Here are some hindrances I see in developing friendships beyond the acquaintanceship level.

1. *Disinterested/alienated people* may have significant psychological problems. These people have a hard time with eye contact and focus, largely because they have such low self-esteem. They really prefer not to meet or talk to anyone else, and when you do try to draw them out by questions, you tend to get a monotone yes and no as a reply.

2. *Self-centered people* like to tell others their troubles. If they get a chance, they will pull out their book of all the things "he" or "she" has done wrong. Though you may have just met, they are ready to go back five years to talk about really personal things.

3. *Superficial people* want to talk only about general

things, and they never reveal any personal issues. They do not know how to ask questions that will draw others out, and if they did, they would be afraid the questions would be turned on them.

4. *Critical people* are simply and plainly negative. They complain incessantly, creating an obviously negative atmosphere. If you, for example, are a critical person, you radiate a negative force around you. When another person approaches you, he picks up your negative vibes. He attributes the negative vibes to the false conclusion that you do not like him. As a result of feeling rejected, he withdraws. You falsely conclude that the withdrawal is rejection, and this "proves" your point: "See, he doesn't like me either, and he doesn't even know me. If he really knew me, he would hate me." So you isolate yourself more and more, and your negative feelings result in your rejecting more people. As you withdraw, you get lonelier and lonelier.

5. *Argumentative people* just want to argue and to criticize. They want to manipulate others for their own good. If you are this kind of person, you will use the people around you for your own benefit. You want others to be available when you are hurting, but you will not be around to help them when they are troubled.

Friendship Enhancers

Ever had someone say to you, "Smile, you're on Candid Camera?" Did you get the message? The glum look on your face needed to be replaced by a smile. I know some people whose physical makeup causes their mouths to turn down. They look angry even when they are neutral. Fortunately, most of us are not so afflicted, so we can more easily smile.

What will a frown do for you that a smile won't? Nothing, except help you develop a reputation for being a grouch. Honestly, if you frown, people will frown back, only confirming to you that nobody likes you. But a smile is also contagious, and it creates a climate in which people can like you.

Do a little experiment. Walk down a reasonably busy street, smiling at people as you walk along. Count the number of smiles you get in contrast to frowns. Notice how many people will actually be so friendly they will wish you a good morning or a good day. You will be amazed at how good you will feel about the smiling response of pure strangers. The Scripture says, "A man who has friends must himself be friendly" (Prov. 18:24 NKJV).

You can do many things to show that you are friendly. I call them "friendship enhancers."

1. *Be a good listener*. Before you make a personal phone call, or sit down with someone you do not know well, make a list of key questions to ask. Occasionally you will run into a totally unresponsive person whose answers are restricted to yes and no, but on the whole you will do very well with this method.

What friendship enhancer did Jesus use when He sat at the well in Samaria and saw a woman come to draw water? That's right, He used questions to draw her out, helping her to develop more significant answers. He was a good listener so that He could be a good helper (see John 4:7–26).

2. *Be concerned for others*. The quickest way to get out of the depths of self-pity is to become involved with others. That means your particular situation should not dominate your thinking and conversation. No matter how bad your situation, others are worse off than you are.

I remember in one episode of the television show "MASH," a man was bemoaning the pain in his leg. A nurse walked by and said, "Maybe you should talk to the guy in the next bed. He doesn't have one." She walked right on, leaving the man to think about something else. Maybe you ought to quit moaning about your hurts and pains and heartaches and start dealing with other people. Take the time to learn about and listen to the hurts of others. It is a very healing experience.

3. *Take the initiative.* So you are scared silly about meeting people. There are bound to be others like you in a group. Go up to someone and say, "My name is _____ and my heart is really beating fast, but I wanted to meet you." Most people will respond favorably. Now fall back on the list of questions you have worked up for such situations. To wait for others to initiate conversation with you is very selfish, so be willing to initiate contacts yourself. That is assuming, of course, that you took the initiative to get into a group setting. These questions do not work well in the solitude of your own home.

4. *Be available.* I know many people who complain because they do not have any friends. They have rarely gone out or had a date, much less had a lasting relationship. They come to meetings ten minutes late and leave five minutes early. Every time someone tries to talk to them, they are on the run. They do not show up at singles' Sunday brunches, hayrides, witnessing outreaches, retreats, or Christmas parties. Yet they want to have friends. In practical terms, they are not available for friendship building. They want a friend but they are not willing to take advantage of opportunities for becoming a friend.

5. *Develop a positive self-image.* To be a friend, you need to develop a positive self-image so that you radiate a positive attitude. As you do that, people will respond positively to you and reinforce your positive self-image. If you are negative about yourself, people will only contribute to that by their responses—and you will convince yourself that nobody likes you.

I don't have the space here to discuss ways in which you can develop a positive self-image, but I recommend an outstanding book by Josh McDowell, *His Image...My Image.* Josh had a terrible self-image problem because he stuttered until he was an adult. Today he is one of the world's top communicators, having spoken to more than seven million students on campuses. What he discovered about his position as a child of God can revolutionize your life.

6. *Show an interest in other people.* Many of us are interested in gaining friends to meet our own needs. Instead, we need to focus on becoming friends to others who need us.

You can do this by determining some basic, general information about someone else. I start with things like where people went to high school, where they were born, and where they work. This level of information can be gained in any public gathering of people, and most people are willing to share it.

The world is truly a small place today, so you may be surprised that the person you are talking to comes from the same area as you do. A couple of men in our city were at a social function when one of them said, "Boy, I remember when I went to fourth grade in _____ ," and he mentioned an obscure town in Oregon. The other man perked up, "What was the name of that town?" They discovered they had both gone through fourth grade in the same classroom. Yet they had worked together for more than five years and not discovered it.

At a conference recently the speaker had been on an aircraft carrier in the South Pacific as a member of the Broken Arrow Squadron. After his message he was talking to another man about it, relating certain events that had happened. Suddenly the other man said, "Hey, I was in that same squadron." He dug out a picture that was probably forty years old of him standing in front of the broken arrow insignia. They discovered that his squadron had replaced the squadron in which the speaker had served. To get this kind of information, you need to become truly interested in other people and ask questions.

7. *Help others.* Is someone in your church group moving? Volunteer to help pack, move, unpack. That kind of helping contact works wonders in developing friendly relationships. You will become friendly not only with the person you are helping but also with the others helping make the move happen. The word will get around that you like helping others, and soon you will have more opportunities for helping/ friendship building experiences.

Some of the best friends you will ever make are handicapped or seniors. Blind people love to have someone read to them. Those in wheelchairs often need help with shopping. Shut-ins require transportation to get to doctors. The elderly in convalescent homes often have no family nearby. You can become Christ's representative to them.

If your problems are the driving force in your life, you make it difficult for people to be friendly with you. The more you isolate yourself, the more you feel nobody likes you. It's a spiral that goes down and down until you have so many problems you have no time or interest in anyone but yourself. To get well, you need to help others. That is part of God's healing process.

8. *Develop a support system.* God created us as social beings. We are built, created, and wired to be with people, but we are also created with a thing called "loneliness." Believe me, loneliness is a positive characteristic because God built it in as part of the basic system. In fact, it was a part of our nature when God created us perfect in Adam before the Fall. God uses it as the motivational force that drives us into relationships with other people and into friendships.

Then, the best solution to loneliness clearly must be marriage! But if that were true, all married people would be happy, and there would be no lonely married people. You know that is not true, because you know of many married people who are extremely lonely.

Loneliness is solved by friendships and relationships. If you are lonely, become part of a singles group, join a group Bible study at church so you can interact with adults of all ages, or join a choir in your community or at church. The smaller the group and the more oriented it is to prayer and Bible study, the stronger it will be as a support group. Some counselors even recommend that if you are in Christian work, you develop a personal "board of directors," a group of three to five who meet with you on a regular basis for prayer and interaction.

A support system is not a one-way street. If you join it merely to benefit yourself, you will be sorely disappointed. Only as you reach out to others in the group will you be accepted and helped. I've seen many takers in these support groups drop out after a few months because they did not feel accepted. Their unwillingness to get involved with others was the wall they pushed in front of them. Learn to reach out to others so you can reach out to your ex.

There is no justification for being unfriendly. That just feeds the negative system. He sues you, you sue him. Back and forth you go as the court system swallows what little financial resources you may have—and the children become the victims of your spite. Only one person needs to become genuinely friendly for the atmosphere to change completely. It is amazing how much people are willing to cooperate with friendly people.

The Biblical Pattern

One of the most poignant passages in Paul's letters is

found in Phillippians 4:2: "I urge Euodia and I urge Syntyche to live in harmony in the Lord." The apostle Paul considered restoring a friendly relationship between fellow Christians so important he included this mention of two women in a letter to the church at Philippi.

Paul had set the biblical pattern in an earlier passage:

If therefore there is any encouragement in Christ, if there is any consolation of love, if there is any fellowship of the Spirit, if any affection and compassion, make my joy complete by being of the same mind, maintaining the same love, united in spirit, intent on one purpose. Do nothing from selfishness or empty conceit, but with humility of mind let each of you regard one another as more important than himself; do not merely look out for your own personal interests, but also for the interests of others (Phil. 2:1-4).

Remember Jim and Bonnie? After being divorced five years, Jim asked Bonnie for a date. Here's how she tells it:

"When Jim asked me to take a drive with him, he took me out to Yosemite Lake. He told me that he had done a lot of praying and felt that the Lord was directing him to make an attempt to be reconciled with me. My stomach was in knots, and I wanted to say no because I disliked him very much. Yet I also felt that if I said no I might condemn him to a life of unspirituality.

"For a while we were simply polite with each other. But we were also having more communication than we had before."

Jim's attempt at being friendly paid off. Within a year he and Bonnie were remarried. In the next chapter we will begin to examine the process of reconciliation, building on the effort to be friendly. Remember, the goal of reconciliation is restoring your relationship with your ex to the friendship level, even if it cannot lead to remarriage.

I'm Trying, My Ex Isn't

Susan had entered the hospital to deliver her third child. In her eighteenth hour in labor the doctor sent Ed, her totally exhausted husband, home to catch some sleep. When he arrived, his attractive sister-in-law offered him a cup of coffee in the kitchen. She had come to take care of the two preschoolers while Susan and Ed were at the hospital.

Ed had always enjoyed being with Kathy, a teacher with ample time to travel and participate in the cultural life of the community. His wife usually talked about household events, but Kathy rambled on about the newest art exhibit, the ballet, and the opera, stretching his mind and enriching his understanding of their community.

As Kathy and Ed chatted, somehow Ed didn't feel so fatigued anymore. What he did not realize was that he was falling into an all-too common trap during a wife's pregnancy and hospital stay.

Only in the ensuing months, when her sister showed signs of pregnancy, did Susan realize what had been going on at home while she gave birth to a son. When Susan confronted Ed, he denied everything, but Kathy could not lie to her sister and told the truth about the short affair. Ed left soon afterward, unable to handle the repeated explosions of anger from Susan as she vented her emotional hurt.

What hope is there that Susan and Ed will be reconciled?

Who should make the first move? Is it really possible for Susan to forgive Ed and be truly reconciled with him despite what he has done? These are questions we will explore together, but you must recognize there are no final answers that fit every situation.

Moving Out of Harmony

Reflect on your experiences in your marriage. You may want to go back all the way to the last days before the wedding. Incredible as it may seem, the first steps to the breakup of a marriage are often taken during the hectic final moments of preparation. Harsh words are spoken, a quarrel is ignited by a difference of opinion over a part of the ceremony—all are entered into the computer that is your mind.

Now think of that first week, the first month, the first year. What happened to build hostility and to drive you away from the line of harmony? Maybe it was the way your spouse treated your mother, how he reacted when an old girlfriend showed up at a party, or how she got into an overlong conversation with an old boyfriend at a church function. The first incident possibly drove you one step off the line of reconciliation; the next, three steps; the next, five. Yet each time you returned to the line of reconciliation because you wanted to make the marriage work.

There is nothing unusual about a series of disagreements that drive a couple to the limits of harmony. As long as they both return to the line of reconciliation within a reasonable length of time, the limits of harmony will not be exceeded.

A Normal Pattern

Turn back to Chapter Three. Figure 3.6 (p.42) shows what happens in a normal marriage. The cycle from argument to resolution may last only one evening, when both are Spirit-led Christians who believe that the sun should not go down on their anger (see Eph. 4:26). Some couples spend time each day to make the effort to deal with anger growing out of differences.

Some couples have a long fuse, and it takes longer for their hostility to develop and to resolve. That is a legitimate, human pattern, which does not change the argue-and-resolve pattern in the illustration. The wave is just longer on the chart. Some issues may take weeks, months, or years to resolve, but the couple can still remain within the limits of harmony.

Conflict Avoidance

Consider the pattern of Jim and Bonnie. To the casual observer they probably did not seem to explode beyond the limits of harmony for the fourteen years of their marriage. Why, when Jim admits he never felt any love for Bonnie?

"I would do anything to avoid conflict," says Bonnie.

Though that attitude avoided an explosion that made them exceed the limits of harmony, it also made the marriage so unexciting for Jim that he developed a relationship outside of marriage. Constant yielding is not resolution.

Meeting Conflict Head-on

Now notice the difference after reconciliation and remarriage, as described by Jim during a testimony he and Bonnie gave at a reconciliation seminar. When asked, "How are things going now that you are married?" Jim said, "Right this moment, not the best. We had just a little bit of an argument coming up today. We don't want anyone to think that just because you get married again all of a sudden things are peaches and cream, and there won't be any problems. There will be, but they can be resolved.

"Bonnie and I have learned how to resolve our conflicts, and we will resolve this one as well. We will not go to bed angry tonight. We will get it straightened out," Jim said.

What Jim is saying is that they will move quickly from argument to resolution. They will not let one issue develop the momentum to propel either of them beyond the limits of harmony. As long as Jim and Bonnie practice this kind of conflict resolution, the graph of their marriage will look like that of a normal marriage.

After the Divorce

How does the chart look when a couple separates and one of them sues for divorce? See Figure 3.7 in Chapter Three (p. 44). The husband and wife typically operated within the limits of harmony for periods of days, months, or years. One day the pressure of growing anger and hostility exploded into such serious disharmony that one of them said, "This is it. I've taken all I can take. I don't need this marriage badly enough to put up with you."

The other person may still be willing to stay within the limits of harmony. In fact, the final decree may be what releases the anger and sends this person out beyond the limits. This is what happened to Bonnie, whose conflict-avoidance techniques, including her church activity, had kept her within the limits of harmony in a loveless marriage. Then Jim left, but not before he told her he had never loved her. She became so angry that she was unwilling to consider any attempt at reconciliation on Jim's part. What could ever motivate her to move back toward the line of reconciliation?

Your Move

The first move back to the line of reconciliation typically comes after the failure of the extramarital relationship that

131

caused the rupture. Jim, for example, had developed a relationship with another teacher that temporarily proved to be a lot more satisfying than his marriage relationship. Since he saw no future in his marriage, he moved out. Yet seven months later he moved back in with Bonnie for a short cycle of reconciliation.

Had Bonnie changed? Not really.

Had Jim's feelings about Bonnie changed? No, they certainly hadn't.

Then why did he move back? Because the relationship with the other teacher had failed to mature, and the relationship with Bonnie was a safe haven to return to while he licked his wounds and regrouped. However, this reconciliation was for the wrong motive, and Jim soon moved out again.

Recycling happens so often in relationships between singles that they almost follow a predictability curve. Boy meets girl, and they "fall in love." They date for a period of time and get physically involved. One day an apparently more exciting prospect crosses the young man's line of vision. He drops Girl 1 and makes a move on Girl 2. He thinks things are going great until one day Girl 2 appears at the basketball game with another guy. Baffled, hurting from the slight, he calls up Girl 1 and asks for a date. If Girl 1 has also developed a new relationship, she will be uninterested in returning to the line of reconciliation and will snub Boy 1.

Different Pressures

If you are the wife in the relationship that has broken up, you face a different pressure to return to the line of reconciliation. Why in the world would Bonnie *let* Jim move back into the house after he destroyed the marriage because of his affair?

In the first place, the wife normally pursues another relationship after divorce out of bitterness and a desire for revenge. "You've made me suffer, so I'll make you suffer. I'll show you that you are not the only one who can develop another relationship." And she does. But the pressure of family members (the children or her parents) and of friends is strong enough to get her back to the line of reconciliation. She often arrives there with the new relationship on one arm in an I'll-show-you attitude, however.

One woman who attended my classes always came with her husband, but she was living with another man at the time. Hypocrisy? No, she just didn't have the courage to hurt the man she was living with. This is often true when emotional bonding has occurred in a new relationship or when the new person clings emotionally. The process of reconciliation can become very complicated.

Disharmony Appears as Harmony

An interesting aspect of this process is that the distance between two people can be so far apart that they are almost in harmony for a period of time. They will carry on business about the house and the investments and discuss the children. They have created so much distance between each other that getting together no longer has the pressure for reconciliation built into it. The spouse is in effect a "stranger" emotionally.

Difficulties with the Decree

Put yourself in the lawyer's place while the couple are cycling in and out of the limits of harmony. Getting anything finally accomplished is virtually impossible.

You get with your client in the proceeding, and he is so distressed that he is ready for counseling or anything that will bring his wife back. He is ready to reconcile, but in talking to the wife, you discover she is far from the line of reconciliation. Knowing that while both parties are in such states you can proceed no further, you throw the file in a drawer.

Two months later she calls up and says, "Hey, I'm ready for some action. Let's get on with the program." You drag out the file, write it up for further activity, and call the husband. By now he is enjoying another relationship and says, "Hang it on your head." So you throw the file back into the drawer, where it sits a few more weeks.

At last you think things have simmered down enough to get some final signatures. You get one of the parties to come in and sign, but there still is no willingness on the part of the other. Months later you get the other party. And just as the whole process is almost finalized, one of them wants to call off the divorce. Is it any wonder lawyers get out of divorce activity?

Stay on the Line!

Some people think that when a spouse goes beyond the limits of harmony, sues for divorce, and gets it, they do not need to seek reconciliation. The feeling is, "After all, I've suffered enough. I deserve my freedom. I've got every right to harbor my resentment and anger." Yet I have seen over and over again that when one of the partners is willing to go back to the line of reconciliation and literally park there, the other will return periodically. Reconciliation *is* possible.

Let the cycle take its course. If you are the one who decides to take the initiative and stick around for a reconciliation, it will be a struggle. You will be tempted to get into a new relationship. A truly alluring person may come along just when you have made up your mind to wait for your spouse to cycle back to the line of reconciliation. While your spouse is out on the town with an apparently exciting new friend, you may be tempted to step out, just out of spite!

Don't give up and don't give in to despair. If you will wait it out, your ex will cycle back. It may be a month, three months, a year, or even longer, but your ex will come back, as certainly as the maple leaves turn color in fall. If a counselor is then brought into the situation, reconciliation can occur. Remember, the aim of reconciliation is to help you to be friendly again and to bring back harmony. Certainly, that is worth the wait.

Mature Christian counseling can help you stay on the line of reconciliation during this time. I know few people who can really wait patiently for anything, and the reassurance and guidance of a counselor you trust can sustain you now. As important as this counsel is, however, the most important counsel will come from above. The Lord is our rock and our fortress and He will lead and guide us (see Pss. 31:3; 73:24).

Cycling Back on Failure

Let's assume you were the ex who waited and your former spouse cycled back into counseling with you. Suddenly your ex left, drifting off into another relationship. Does that free you? Not really, because your ex will almost certainly cycle back again and again. The chances of reconciliation increase each time this happens—as long as you are still at the line of reconciliation.

In analyzing both John and Judy's and Jim and Bonnie's patterns after divorce, we see them getting back together time and time again. The fact that Judy had not remarried by the time John had the motorcycle accident, committed his life to Christ, and came back for reconciliation made remarriage possible. That Bonnie was still available six years after Jim had divorced her made remarriage possible in their case.

I encourage people to make a commitment to go to the line of reconciliation and sit there for a while. Dig in and say, "Hey, I am committed to being single for a while, and I am going to put all potential new relationships out of my life. I am going to concentrate on a good same-sex friend.

"Yes, I will be friendly with the opposite sex, but I will not cross the line of friendship into relationship with anyone else. I will be available for reconciliation and will work on putting my life back together right here on this line of reconciliation. I will become a reconciler."

That is tough to do. It takes committed men and women who are willing to put aside their personal desires and say, "Hey, I am willing to work at this thing. I am willing to dig in and make a fight of it." (See Fig. 10.1 for how this commitment looks on the graph for reconciliation.)

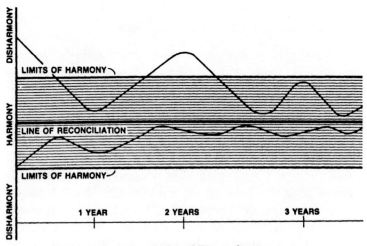

Fig. 10.1 Cycles of Reconciliation
Reconciling

If you are at the separated stage, I want to say that I do not consider you free to walk away from your marriage until you have sincerely attempted reconciliation. The duration of that is not the twenty minutes it takes him to pick up his clothes. I am talking about months, even years.

The price of that kind of commitment to reconciliation is high. Part of the price is your personal freedom. You may see what you consider the opportunity of a lifetime slip away in terms of a new relationship. You may miss the opportunity to meet the prince or princess of your life. I can assure you that as soon as you make that commitment, the best-looking, most marvelous person you have ever met in your whole life will come drifting into your life. You will look for every escape clause in the commitment you made. But like the Nazarite in the Old Testament who made his vow, you have made a commitment and you need to keep it. Nobody wants to hear that, and I hear few counselors or advisors saying that. But someone needs to say it, and people need to start doing it if more couples are going to be reconciled.

It's Useless

What if it does not work? I admit that staying at the line of reconciliation may not work. Your ex may decide to have nothing to do with you. If that happens, you will have a clear conscience—the ability to stand before people and God and say, "I gave it my best shot. Drawing on the power of the Holy Spirit living in me, I was willing to forgive, to forget, and to wait out my ex."

That in itself is extremely valuable in starting another relationship. Would you feel more comfortable marrying a person who has done this and waited two years or one who walked away from his wife the first time she messed up and never attempted to be reconciled to her?

What will help break the cycle? After years of working in the area of divorce recovery and reconciliation, I am convinced the most effective remedy is spiritual renewal on the part of one or the other or both. Someone has to say, "I will obey God. I will do what He tells me to do in His Word."

That's what both John and Jim did. Each of them said, "It's not right. What I am doing is contrary to God's will for me and my family. Like the prodigal son I will return and try to re-establish the relationship." Because God was their ally, their ex's were willing to make the effort, and God gave the "increase."

What does the Bible say about reconciliation? One day the apostle Peter came to Jesus with the question, "Lord, how often shall my brother sin against me and I forgive him? Up to seven times?" (Matt. 18:21). (If this had happened in the 1980s, I would immediately suspect he was talking about a divorce proceeding. The list of transgressions by either spouse typically exceeds seven!)

Jesus responded to Peter, "I do not say to you, up to seven times, but up to seventy times seven" (18:22). That list would exceed even the longest lawyer's list in most divorce proceedings! Later, Jesus stated that divorce had been written into the Mosaic legal code only because of the hardness of the human heart (see Matt. 19:7–9).

If forgiving our spouse "seventy times seven" is God's path to the line of reconciliation, why do even Christians have such a tough time parking on that line? To reveal our problem, Jesus told a parable of a king and his slaves, which I suggest you read in your favorite translation in Matthew 18:23–35.

What was the "wicked" slave's sin? He was forgiven his enormous debt by a generous king, but he refused to forgive a minor debtor and threw him in prison. What was the king's reaction when he heard of the wicked slave's inhumanity? He was so incensed at the unforgiving spirit of the wicked slave that he handed the slave over to the "torturers."

What is Jesus' application? "So shall My heavenly Father also do to you, if each of you does not forgive his brother from your heart" (Matt. 18:35). I see a lot of divorced singles who have been handed over to the "torturers"! They have received total, unconditional forgiveness from their King—God Himself—but they are not willing to forgive those who have sinned against them.

Our Debt Was Forgiven

All of us carried this enormous burden of sins committed against our heavenly Father. We were worthy of being divorced from God forever. Yet He broke down the wall of separation—of divorce—and forgave us our sin because Jesus died on the cross in our place. He parked on the line of reconciliation until we cycled back to it when tired of our sin. The apostle Paul concluded,

For it was the Father's good pleasure...through Him to reconcile all things to Himself, having made peace through the blood of His cross; through Him, I say, whether things on earth or things in heaven. And although you were formerly alienated and hostile in mind, engaged in evil deeds, yet He has now reconciled you in His fleshly body through death, in order to present you before Him holy and blameless and beyond reproach (Col. 1:19–22).

If that is what our King has done for us, how then should we react to the "debt" of a spouse? Should we throw the debtor in the prison of unreconciliation, being forever unforgiving of the debt? Or should we return to the line of reconciliation in order to avoid the horror of being consigned to our particular outer darkness by our eternal King, Jesus Christ?

The fact is that none of us has the inner resources to park for long on the line of reconciliation. We need a support system, and the best support system is Jesus Christ living in us through the Holy Spirit. Take time to read carefully and thoughtfully Paul's letters to the Ephesians, Philippians, and Colossians. Catch the can-do spirit of this man in prison. Learn to say with him, "I can do all things through Him [Christ] who strengthens me" (Phil. 4:13).

In the next chapter we are going to discuss the unthinkable for many singles I counsel—remarriage. We are going to examine the steps that have worked in the lives of numerous couples who are now remarried following years of divorce.

To Try Again
or Not to Try Again

A friend of mine spent several years in Connecticut. An avid gardener, he dug and tilled a plot for vegetables every year. The first year he almost injured his back by carrying away all the rocks he dug up.

Suppose you had arrived one spring as he was beginning to dig. You noticed he was working over a fresh patch of grass instead of turning over the previous year's plot. What would you have said? I suspect you would have called him foolish, at the very least.

That is exactly what many formerly married singles do over and over again. They prepare new "soil" for another relationship when they have an older soil (a former relationship) with a lot less rocks buried underground. A lot of effort has gone into removing rocks in the former relationship, making it a lot easier to become fruitful again.

It is true that in the interval new rocks have worked their way to the surface, even in the most deeply dug soils. Some are surprisingly large. Despite that, there is still no comparison between the number of rocks in the old, dug-over plot (the old relationship) and the number in the new undug area (the new relationship).

Take a look around you. List your friends who are desperately reaching out for new relationships, when considerably less effort would cause them to be reconciled to their former spouses. Would they not be better off working the old soil, especially if they got some help with the digging from an expert gardener—a counselor? Certainly even the old soil will produce a kink or two in the back from the effort, but it is nothing compared to the pain caused by the prolonged effort in working a new plot—a new relationship.

Reconciliation Is Biblical

One of the hardest things to get across to a formerly married single is that reconciliation is not an *option* for the Christian intent on obeying God. Remember Jim and Bonnie? When Jim was asked at a seminar, "What brought you to the point of reconciliation?" he replied, "I had done a lot of praying about it. I felt the Lord was directing me to at least make an attempt to reconcile with Bonnie. If I wanted to be in God's will, I had to make the effort."

You see, Jim recognized that Jesus' mission on earth was one of reconciliation, as revealed in Colossians 1:20, "And through Him to reconcile all things to Himself, having made peace through the blood of His cross; through Him, I say, whether things on earth or things in heaven." The One who died on the cross to reconcile us to God also promotes reconciliation while living in us as our Lord and Savior.

The practical outworking of this is illustrated in Paul's letter to the Philippians, where that marvelous passage about being anxious for nothing is preceded by that admonition we looked at earlier: "I urge Euodia and I urge Syntyche to live in harmony in the Lord" (Phil. 4:2). Imagine coming to church one Sunday morning, and the pastor reads a letter from an evangelist who held a crusade in town a year earlier. Suddenly you start to feel your face getting red as the pastor reads, "I urge Tim and Sherri to live in harmony in the Lord." You have been unwilling to move back to the line of reconciliation, and word somehow reached the evangelist. That is exactly what happened in the church in Philippi. The apostle Paul felt it was vital for Christians to be reconciled to one another.

Reconciliation Is Your Choice

Let me emphasize that reconciliation is your choice, just as Christ decided to die for us to reconcile us to God while we were His enemies: "But God demonstrates His own love toward us, in that while we were yet sinners, Christ died for us" (Rom. 5:8). He chose to come to the line of reconciliation and stay there until we turned to Him. In the same way you need to move toward the line of reconciliation when there is as yet no hope your ex will ever come to it too.

Bonnie confesses that she really had no interest in reconciling with Jim because of her intense dislike of him. Jim knew this, but he persisted anyway. Even though he clumsily made one mistake after another, his commitment to God's principle of reconciliation won the day.

Reconciliation for What?

When I use the word *reconciliation* with formerly married singles, they inevitably recoil. They immediately assume I want them to remarry their former spouses. Though I know it will happen in some cases, I am under no illusion that this is a reasonable goal for all. Some former spouses have already remarried. Others will never achieve the spiritual, emotional, and financial maturity to become good candidates for remarriage. My goal is their reconciliation to the friendship level, and anything beyond that is a bonus for all concerned.

For this reason I propose a friendship commitment as a first step in reconciliation, that is, a return to a normal human basis in your interaction with your ex, even though that person has remarried. Agreement to this step will mean a spiritual renewal for some of you. By nature we are at enmity not only with God but also with others. You may not ever want to see anything good happen to your ex.

Reconciliation in Four Stages

I have developed a reconciliation process that takes individuals and couples through four stages.

1. *Reconciliation Commitment:* One individual chooses to sign a six-month agreement to stay on the line of reconciliation. This allows for growth and maturity and limits dating or other activities with the opposite sex that could lead to a relationship.

2. *Friendship Instruction:* Two people choose to sign a four-month agreement to be friendly with each other. No relational activity is permitted, and they are limited to activities with a same-sex friend.

3. *Reconciliation Discussion:* A couple commit to examine their relationship and improve harmony for a period of four months, meeting every other week, doing homework assignments, limiting physical involvement, and getting to know one another again as friends. The study material appears at the end of this book.

4. *Relationship Instruction:* A couple, along with an instructor, choose to sign a four-month agreement to meet every other week, do homework assignments, and limit the physical involvement to avoid immorality. This instructional material is in a separate workbook.

5. *Premarital Counseling:* An engaged couple commit to two months of weekly meetings with a counselor to prepare themselves for marriage. This program should be available through a local church in your area.

The Reconciliation Commitment

For those of you serious about reconciliation, I propose a reconciliation commitment for a period of six months. This commits you to 180 days of toughing it out on the line of reconciliation with your ex. The commitment is outlined in Figure 11.1.

Fig. 11.1 Six-month Reconciliation Commitment

Reconcile: 1. to cause to cease hostility or opposition; 2. to cause to accept or be resigned to something not desired; 3. to harmonize or settle; 4. to restore.

1. These guidelines are recommended to help bring spiritual and emotional growth and stability to individuals who are in transition from the following areas:

   a. Healing from a hurtful relationship
   b. Present separation
   c. Recently divorced

2. I agree to keep my schedule open for

   a. Home Bible study
   b. Christian fellow-ship
   c. Self development through Christian counsel
   d. Discovering growth possibilities

3. My goal is to remain open to reconciliation with my spouse or ex-spouse for a period of six months. This means I choose no one-to-one dating during this time. I will not do anything with the opposite sex that I cannot comfortably do with a same-sex friend.

I can do all things through Christ who strengthens me (Phil. 4:13 NKJV).

4. My desire is to know what God's will is for my life and to develop a strong Christian environment through Christian fellowship.

My son, never forget the things I've taught you. If you want a long and satisfying life, closely follow my instructions. Never tire of loyalty and kindness. Hold these virtues tightly. Write them deep within your heart. If you want favor with both God and man, and a reputation for good judgment and common sense, then trust the Lord completely; don't ever trust yourself. In everything you do, put God first, and he will direct you and crown your efforts with success (Prov. 3:1–6 TLB).

5. The above guidelines are to allow God sufficient time to work in my life, and I look forward eagerly to discovering His plan for me.

6. This commitment will be kept from _____ to
_____.

_____

Signature

_____

Date

At the very least when you have completed the six-month commitment, you will be more stable, more in control emotionally, better off financially, and a lot more established in your relationships. Should you later choose, and be biblically eligible for, marriage to someone else, you will have a far greater chance of success.

Friendship Instruction

If you have enough harmony in the relationship to get serious, the next step is friendship instruction. This program is self-monitoring and has limited time and physical guidelines to prevent too rapid advancement into a relationship. As you look over Figure 11.2, you can review the goals and guidelines. Remember that this can be used between same-sex friends as well. This is the real test of friendship. If you are able to complete this with your ex-mate, you can move on to the next level of commitment.

_____

Fig. 11.2. Friendship Instruction

Goals:

1. To promote our spiritual maturity through encouraging each other in worship and service to Jesus Christ.

2. To develop agape love.

3. To learn to control our physical, emotional, and mental habits.

4. To build trust, integrity, and transparency.

5. To allow same-sex and opposite-sex friends to practice and build quality friendships.

146

Limits: No physical touching (hand-holding, arm-in-arm).

Time:

1. Four months.
2. Twenty to thirty hours maximum per month.
3. Group time to count as one-fourth time alone.
4. Phone time as full time after a half hour.

Things to Do:

1. Share goals, needs, victories.
2. Bible study, prayer, memorization.
3. Read and outline *Friends and Friendships*, by Jerry White.

Things to Avoid:

1. All talk of relationships and marriage.
2. Too much contact with engaged or married couples.
3. Intimate, cozy atmosphere.
4. Romantic movies, gifts, cards, compliments.
5. Self-absorption.

Date _____

Signed _____

Signed _____

To even agree to this step will mean a spiritual renewal for some people. By nature we are full of enmity against God, and we also love to hold grudges against others. We don't even want to see anything good happen to our ex's. They don't deserve normalization of the relationship with us.

Jim put it this way, "If you are thinking about getting back together again, you have to put the Lord first. I am definitely convinced of that. Bonnie and I would never have gotten back together if we had not put the Lord first. On my own I could never have loved her. There are many things in her that just absolutely turn me off. The love I have for Bonnie is a gift of God I received after I committed myself to living in obedience to Him. If you put the Lord first and really seek His will, He will, through the Holy Spirit, resolve the differences between you."

For this reason I propose a friendship commitment as a step in reconciliation. The goal is to return to a normal human basis in your interaction with your ex, even though that person has remarried.

Relationship Instruction

The process of reconciliation can be very frustrating, and this material can be effective in keeping the relationship on track! The prerequisites are listed in Figure 11.3, and the complete program is available in the workbook also titled *Too Close, Too Soon*, published by Thomas Nelson. Over the last few years this has provided the steppingstone for many couples to bring their relationships back into the area of harmony.

Fig. 11.3. Relationship Instruction

Prerequisites:

1. You must have a strong and consistent friendship with the freedom to hold each other physically.

2. You must have the willingness to meet for eight sessions, which will be scheduled every other week for approximately four months.

3. All subjects, assignments, and discussions are to be confidential to protect the integrity of the relationship.

4. No wedding proposal or date is to be discussed (if this has already taken place, you must be willing to stop discussion). This includes discussing which season (next spring) or month (next September).

5. You must not *talk* or even *think* about marriage. This is to protect the relationship from any unrealistic expectations.

6. You must be willing to become mutually exclusive (no one-on-one time with anyone of the opposite sex). This means no luncheons, gifts, notes, cards. If there is another relationship going on, be willing to tell the person involved about the present commitment and keep it at a friendship level.

7. Each of you must be willing to do one to two hours of homework each week and schedule one to two hours a week to discuss the homework.

8. Even if the relationship does not keep going, the commitment to this relationship instruction must continue for the eight sessions.

9. You must agree to keep the following limits on time spent alone together:

First month: 20 hours
Second month: 30 hours
Third month: 40 hours
Fourth month: 50 hours

One-on-one time is counted hour for hour; group time is divided by four; phone time is counted when the conversation lasts over a half hour. This is to be kept on a monthly time chart, giving a total of 140 hours in four months.

10. You must be honest about the physical part of the relationship:

(1) Look
(2) Touch
(3) Lightly holding hands
(4) Constantly holding hands
(5) Light kiss
(6) Strong kiss
(7) French kiss
(8) Fondling breasts
(9) Fondling sexual organs
(10) Sexual intercourse

11. If your relationship goes to eight or beyond, you will be asked to do additional homework by filling out the "Gaining Moral Freedom" worksheet.

12. The man must be willing to contact the instructor if the number reaches eight. If the man does not, it is the woman's responsibility. This is to help save your relationship.

13. Each of you must pay any fees required for books and tests.

14. You must sign a written commitment of these prerequisites.

Signed _____

Remarriage as a Goal

If remarriage is your goal, as it was with John and Judy, Jim and Bonnie, what "rocks" need to be cleared out of the way first?

1. Am I, Under God, Free to Remarry?

We covered this in Chapter Eight. Christians are not automatically free to remarry their former spouses. If neither of you has married someone else since your divorce, you are obviously eligible to remarry from the biblical perspective. Yet if either one of you has married again and that marriage did not work out, you are not free to remarry.

What is so wrong with remarrying a former spouse who has been married since your divorce? Here is God's view on it, as expressed in Deuteronomy 24:4: "Her former husband who sent her away is not allowed to take her again to be his wife, since she has been defiled; for that is an abomination before the LORD, and you shall not bring sin on the land which the LORD your God gives you as an inheritance." Thus if you remarry the spouse who has married again and divorced again, you are committing an abomination in God's eyes.

Unfortunately, many people do not consider this issue until it is too late. Typically, singles will ask that question when they are still outside a relationship. They will search the Scriptures and do homework on the issue. Once they have become friends with a member of the opposite sex, they will still ask the question, but they will usually do less biblical study of the issue. When the friendship has progressed to the relationship stage, they no longer seem to care.

Should marriage take place, the question often comes up again, and they have to deal with it in the context of their new marriage. I have had couples come to me during the first month of their marriage and say, "You know, I don't think I was scripturally free to remarry. I need to divorce this woman (or man) and go back and remarry my first wife (or husband)." That is a tough time to lay Deuteronomy 24:4 on them! Now, they have to make this marriage work.

2. Am I Spiritually Stable and Growing?

Both of you need to be able to stand alone spiritually and not be dependent on the other. Yet how do you achieve that spiritual maturity?

Assuming you have both made a personal commitment to Jesus Christ as Savior and Lord, the first step is regular church attendance. One woman told me, "I would reconcile, but each time I start the reconciliation process he is going to a different church. He joins a church during the reconciliation process, and stops going as soon as we are reconciled. I've been through that cycle three times."

I recommend that you attend church consistently but go to the services separately, not together. I also suggest you attend different Sunday school classes, so neither of you goes merely to be with the other but to genuinely learn the Word and to worship. Going to church together is no clear indicator you are going to make it in marriage again.

One of the things we do in relationship instruction is a spiritual evaluation checklist. Are you reading the Bible, and having a quiet time with the Lord and a daily prayer time? Are you studying the Bible when you are together, discovering what God is saying to both of you? Do you pray together?

I don't mean that you need to do this every day. That is an ideal often presented to us, but it is unrealistic. For example, my wife rarely prays aloud when I pray with her. Yet she has a close, devout spiritual relationship and a well-developed private prayer life. To ask her to pray along with me is just not her style—that is not the balance we have with each other.

My wife is much more concerned about giving financially

than I am. She will say, "Don't you think we ought to give money to this project?" I normally agree; I just do not think of it first. So she takes the lead in that.

In our relationship with our neighbors, she is much more effective than I am. Yet I am more effective in witnessing for Christ with strangers. So we each exercise the gifts God has given us. I feel blessed that we recognize these special gifts so that we can balance each other's strengths and weaknesses.

You as a couple will have to work out your own balance. There simply are no hard and fast rules for spiritual growth, even though there are some indicators that I watch for when counseling a couple planning to remarry.

3. Am I Emotionally Stable Enough?

Are your emotions stable enough to cope not only with your mood swings but also with those of your spouse?

Remember Bonnie's experience after divorce, an all-too typical pattern? She reports, "I'd go on crying jags, saying I am not worthy for anyone to love." She buried herself in her work at school, at church, and at home with the children. As the years went by, she gradually gained self-confidence. She learned to like herself and to be her own person.

During her marriage to Jim, Bonnie had looked to Jim for emotional support. Since he did not feel any love for her, that was not available. Her craving for it, however, caused her to do anything to avoid conflict since she thought that might bring Jim around. After the divorce, she initially depended on the children for emotional support. She was ready for remarriage only when she was no longer dependent on them or anyone else for self-worth.

The apostle John revealed how closely spiritual maturity is tied to emotional maturity:

Little children, let us stop just *saying* we love people; let us *really* love them, and *show it* by our *actions*. Then we will know for sure, by our actions, that we are on God's side, and our consciences will be clear, even when we stand before the Lord. But if we have bad consciences and feel that we have done wrong, the Lord will surely feel it even more, for he knows everything we do.

But, dearly loved friends, if our consciences are clear, we can come to the Lord with perfect assurance and trust, and get whatever we ask for because we are obeying him and doing the things that please him (1 John 3:18–22 TLB).

Notice how closely the way we feel is tied to our relationship with God. The emotional release of having a good conscience, of knowing we are living in the will of God, of experiencing His love flowing through us to others, is truly incredible. Until that happens to each of us, we are not able to help a spouse when our help is required.

4. Am I Financially in a Position to Remarry?

Two cannot live as cheaply as one. In an earlier chapter I focused on the need to develop financial stability after a divorce. I mentioned the excesses in spending typical of most new singles. Since inadequate financial resources, or excessive financial demands by one spouse, are a key contributing factor to divorce, you will need to have developed self-control in spending habits.

Yet it is not enough to have day-by-day spending under control. Many singles spend themselves into heavy debt just before or after divorce. This will hang like a sword of Damocles over their heads when they remarry. Just when your spouse wants a new kitchen range, a sofa, or carpeting, you may have a balloon payment of some kind. At such a time, the lack of financial discipline in the past can come to haunt your new marriage relationship.

"We'll manage," you say. I have seen too many marital disasters as a result of that attitude. Get your financial house in order before you remarry, or stay at the friendship level with your former spouse. The same goes for you who might have ideas about marrying someone other than your ex. Only a fool would drive onto a bridge seriously weakened by a flooding river. That is exactly what you would be doing if you married with the financial substructure weakened by poor financial management.

5. What Is Our Relationship Like?

You have completed the friendship instruction period. Yet what is really happening in your relationship? Are you moving forward? Is there a chemistry, that extra pizzazz that says you have a special relationship that can withstand the arrows and slings of misfortune? Are you coasting, or are you constantly working at improving your relationship?

Sometimes a relationship will grow like mad for a while and suddenly grind to a halt, while both do all kinds of other interesting things. One day one of them suggests marriage, and because it sounds great, they settle on a wedding date. Yet their relationship has actually degenerated into a holding position.

You see, the normal pattern in marriage is to separate. That is also true in a relationship. Both of you have to work at it until one of you dies or leaves. To be truly successful when you remarry, you need to have a vibrant, growing relationship before the wedding.

Concern about a growing relationship inevitably involves the children. During the initial period after separation and divorce, children try to keep Dad and Mom together. They know how to act right, and they want their parents to do so too. In fact, in my experience most parents would be better off if they listened to their children during that period.

Once a number of years have passed, the children may become a significant barrier to their parents' remarrying. (Of course, their parents should remarry only if biblically permitted to do so.) Children should not be permitted to control the reconciliation process. Yes, they need to be informed and to be aware of the changing dynamics in the relationship, but their consent should not be solicited or their blessing asked for.

The quality of your relationship as man and woman, as husband and wife, is far more important than how your children feel at the prospect of your remarrying. The children will normally be gone in several years, but your marital relationship can last another thirty or forty years.

Another significant factor is the sheer numbers involved in trying to control a relationship. The more people you get into a developing relationship, the more difficult it is for reconciliation to happen and for the relationship to mature. Normally, allowing several children into the process will destroy any hope of the parents making it together again. So I try to keep the children isolated from the relationship building process when I counsel couples in these situations.

One of the things that does have to happen is that the children have to accept the reality of the reconciliation and remarriage. Sometimes this may mean postponing marriage several months so that Ralph will realize he can throw a fit without having any effect on the reconciliation process. You are going ahead with plans to remarry, and he had better accept that.

Premarital Counseling

Okay, you have been through friendship instruction and relationship instruction. You have achieved reconciliation with your former spouse with the aid of a counselor. You are able to answer positively the questions I have raised. Your children are on board for this new phase in their life. Now what?

Premarital counseling.

"You've got to be kidding," you say. "Friendship and relationship instruction, and now you expect us to go through premarital counseling? We were married to each other for twelve years. What can we learn from premarital counseling? Let's just get married."

This attitude reveals that you have come full cycle. It seems that failure makes you an expert on marriage. The impulse is to repeat the same mistake again and rush the whole process. Take the time to get all the help you can. Remember, time is your ally, not your enemy.

Every couple obviously will have a different approach and a different ceremony. John and Judy quietly headed for Reno and were remarried.

"Looking back, I believe we made a mistake, but we were so anxious to get remarried," says John.

Jim and Bonnie took the opposite route. They took four months of relationship instruction and two months of premarital counseling. Then they invited everyone in the church to the renewal of their vows.

"We had a simple but large celebration. Everyone was so excited. My son gave me away. There was hardly a dry eye in the place when Jim Talley preached a sermon on reconciliation," reports Bonnie.

Equipped with their newfound insight into what makes a marriage successful and knit together by their love relationship developed during the year before remarriage, John and Judy have now been remarried six years and Jim and Bonnie more than two years. In fact, John and Judy lead a class in reconciliation at their church and are assisting other couples in the process of reconciliation. Figure 11.4 shows what happens when remarriage is achieved.

That is too idyllic, you say. You have been telling about John and Judy, Jim and Bonnie, but my ex and I are so far apart there is no hope of reconciliation, much less remarriage.

Let me tell you about Harry and Nadine. He was black and she was white. Both were believers, and when their relationship matured, they went through our premarital counseling program. Everyone had high hopes that even the racial barriers had been successfully overcome.

A few months after the wedding, the marriage began to come unglued. His solution for conflict was to withdraw and be quiet. Her reaction was to attack and yell. They drove the relationship to the limits of harmony, and after only eight months, they separated. The first three weeks

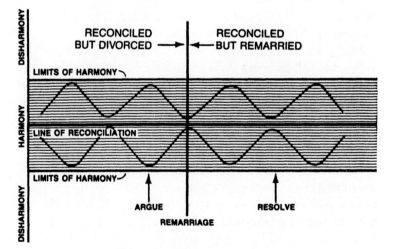

Fig. 11.4. Cycles of Reconciliation
Harmony or Remarriage

they did not see each other at all. Even when their daughter was born, the relationship remained in disharmony. Both of them sought counsel and spent the time growing spiritually.

Harry committed himself to being the reconciler and went to the line of reconciliation. For the next eighteen months the only encouragement he got was a quick trip to the line of reconciliation by Nadine as she gave him an unfelt apology for her attitude, then she left the limits of harmony again.

The most discouraging thing for Harry was that Nadine pursued the divorce and it became final. He stayed on the line for five more months without any encouragement! Finally Nadine called and asked if Harry would like to see his daughter, who was almost six months old. After counsel and growth they renewed their relationship and decided after nine months of being divorced to remarry each other.

Because he was willing to work at it, they were reconciled. They have now been remarried more than seven years. They have done very well at reconciling what appeared to be an irreconcilable relationship. They effectively dealt with the failure of their early relationship, as well as overcoming the racial issues involved.

Harry and Nadine are only one example of the truly unbelievable things being done by people committed to reconciliation. Their example is a challenge to others to be as committed to reconciliation.

Do Remarriages Succeed?

Yes and no. They are just like first marriages in that couples willing to put in the time and effort, each partner willing to give 100 per cent, do very well. But those who do not want to face the responsibility and to work hard at it fail. Such people would fail no matter who they married. And who is to say that marriage to someone else is guaranteed to be better than to a former spouse?

In remarriage, there are no hidden flaws. You both know the whole truth. In a new marriage partner you may need a few years to learn the hidden flaws, and then it is too late to go back! It is not as important to find that special person as it is to *be* that special person.

Long-term Reconciliation

Okay, so remarriage is a serious option. What guarantee is there that the marriage will make it the second time around? Where do you get the glue to make reconciliation stick?

"Commitment," says John, and his wife Judy quickly agrees. "Sometimes commitment is the only thing that keeps us together."

John and Judy speak from more than six years of experience after they were remarried. They were initially married nine years; then they were separated and divorced six years before they remarried.

"It starts with your commitment to the Lord. As believers we commit to Him no matter what, and that is exactly what we have had to do in our marriage," says John. "We have gone through some very trying times. Judy has had a difficult time on the job, with a difficult boss. We have a sixteen-year-old son going on twenty-one.

"When things get rough we have to sit down and go through the act of forgiving each other. There are tears and there is joy. We see our marriage as a process of the everyday, but we have the Lord helping us work it through. By His grace we have been able to honor our commitment to each other."

I hope you understand by now that reconciliation is not easy. If it were, John Mark would have accompanied Paul and Barnabas on their second missionary journey, Joseph would have identified himself to his brothers the first time he saw them, and Jesus would not have had to die on the cross for us to reconcile us to God.

Joseph's commitment to God is revealed in his response to the advances of the wife of Potiphar, "How then could I do this great evil, and sin against God?" (Gen. 39:9). Paul's commitment to God is clear from his statement: "I have been crucified with Christ; and it is no longer I who live, but Christ lives in me; and the life which I now live in the flesh I live by faith in the Son of God, who loved me, and delivered Himself up for me" (Gal. 2:20). That kind of commitment to the indwelling Christ made it impossible for him to hold a lifetime grudge against John Mark and made it possible for reconciliation to take place and Mark to become "useful" to Paul once more.

Of Jesus, the apostle Paul wrote,

For it was the Father's good pleasure for all the fulness to dwell in Him, and through Him to reconcile all things to Himself, having made peace through the blood of His cross; through Him, I say, whether things on earth or things in heaven. And although you were formerly alienated and hostile in mind, engaged in evil deeds, yet He has now reconciled you in His fleshly body through death, in order to present you before Him holy and blameless and beyond reproach (Col. 1:19–22).

What Shape Commitment?

Flowing out of His commitment to us, He will help us establish that kind of commitment to our spouses. Yet what shape does that commitment really take? John shares that this commitment to God and Judy is expressed in three ways in his life.

"I find that we need to get into the Word of God. Our relationship needs to be Word-centered. There we discover what He can do for us and what it means to obey Him," says John. "When we have shared an especially close time of worship with the Lord, we've both come away renewed. We find we cannot do it alone—it is a shared experience. We find that the Lord speaks to us both at the same time.

"Of course, we need to apply what we have learned, and that is the second step in our commitment to God and each other. We need to work out in our life what we have learned. That is very special to me, because it makes the Lord real to me."

Remember, this is the man who did not make a commitment to God until after a motorcycle accident reminded him how close death is to us. The spiritual maturity evident in what he said started to come one year before he and Judy were reconciled, and it has flowered during the years they have been remarried. As Judy says, "If someone had told me six or seven years ago what John is doing now I would have said it was impossible."

Commitment to getting into the Word of God together and to working out in the marriage relationship the implications of obedience to God's Word is tied to a third commitment.

Reconciliation Means Listening

"We have been doing some special study on communication in marriage. We've learned a lot from Norman Wright's book, *Communication: Key to Your Marriage,* and another of his books, *The Family that Listens*. We found that we were often listening with our mouths, not our ears, so we are now making a conscious effort to hear what the other person is really saying. We certainly did not do that before our divorce," John says.

The Primordial Enemy

Probably the most underrated factor in the success or failure of a Christian marriage, and that includes remarriage, is the role of the enemy, Satan. The apostle Peter used colorful language in describing his activities: "Your adversary, the devil, prowls about like a roaring lion, seeking someone to devour" (1 Pet. 5:8). John and Judy found this particularly true when they set about establishing a truly Christian home.

"When we were non-Christians we were not harassed nearly as much," says John. "Since our remarriage we have had to ask ourselves, 'Who do I want to win? Who is pulling the string on what is happening to us?' I focus on that when something happens that has the potential to pull us apart. We want Christ to come out the winner in our life."

That focus, of course, calls for the kind of strategy Peter recommended after his description of Satan: "But resist him, firm in your faith, knowing that the same experiences of suffering are being accomplished by your brethren who are in the world" (1 Pet. 5:9).

This enemy capitalizes on the natural forces in a marriage that would drive us apart. If he can get us to neglect each other's needs for spiritual fellowship, let us forget to truly listen to each other and communicate what is going on inside of us, and con us into letting disagreements mount, he knows the natural forces will take over. He doesn't even need to tempt us to unfaithfulness—it will happen naturally while we are off guard.

Look Out for Rocks

What are some of the trouble spots, the rocks in the soil of marriage? What kinds of experiences can cause significant problems in marriage? I find that some of them are normal for every marriage, but there are a few that tend to crop up more often in remarriage.

1. Overlooking Built-in Needs

In the euphoria of being together again, it is easy for the husband and wife to overlook each other's basic, built-in needs. Research has revealed that the greatest need of the man is for significance, which he tends to get from what he is doing and what he is. The woman, on the other hand, is far more concerned about security, which she interprets to a great extent in terms of dollars.

The man is truly concerned about his job and his family. During separation and divorce, he is in real difficulty because of this anxiety. If in the process of getting a divorce he also loses his job, he is in serious trouble. He can become depressed and sink into almost total despair. A man simply cannot live that way for long.

The woman is in desperate need of security, which is the female's drive mechanism. It means dollars, but dollars alone are not enough security for a woman. Emotional commitment and time spent with her are also involved in her security system. What I believe here does not come from any scientific study, but in my observations and counseling experience I have consistently found that 50 per cent of the woman's security system is dollars, 25 per cent is tied up in how much her husband is committed to her, and the other 25 per cent is tied to how much time he spends with her.

If a man says he is committed to his wife but does not spend any time with her, she can function at 75 per cent if he supports her financially. Some women have learned to do that with their highly aggressive, success-oriented husbands who spend little time with them.

Harder to live with is the husband who supports his wife financially and gives her time, but is not committed to her. Her radar constantly sends her danger signals because of his involvement with other women. That kind of emotional stress can wreak havoc in a marriage.

Husbands, heed my words. You will put the greatest stress on your relationship with your wife after remarriage if you do not give her a financial base to live on. You may be committed to her and give her your time, but that is not enough. I know you can live in a log cabin in the middle of nowhere, shoot everything for dinner, buy ten pounds of salt, and get along. But your wife wants the electric bill, the gas bill, and the mortgage payment paid on time every month.

In a healthy relationship both of you are involved in tradeoffs. Sometimes you will give up some of your significance so she can have more security; sometimes she will give up some security to give you significance. The key is to learn to balance that in your interaction with each other. And once you agree on a tradeoff, stick to it.

About seventeen years ago, my wife and I were excited that God had called us to commit our lives to serving people by going into the ministry. I was trained as an engineer, but we agreed that if I went into the ministry, it would be a highly significant thing for me. Yet it would cost us financially, so I would gain and she would lose. Over a lifetime I would gain significance, but my reduced earning capacity would affect her security.

We made some other decisions about school when we first got married. One was that I could do whatever I wanted with my life as long as I supported the family while doing it. If I wanted to go to school, great, but we lived on what I made. That was the family budget. Anything she earned she could spend as she desired. Neither of us would commit to purchases that would require payments.

What did this mean in practical terms? For me, it meant that I took ten years to get my bachelor's degree. I worked all the time, and we raised three children during those years. I could have gotten it in three years, but I would have come out of school with a debt of $20,000 and a wife who had pulled out all her hair from frustration.

When you remarry, do not play around with the wife's security or reduce the husband's significance. If you use that as one of the ground rules in marriage, you will avoid an amazingly high amount of friction.

2. Digging Up the Past

One of the biggest temptations after remarriage is to dig up the past when you get into a fight. There's the time you failed to show up at your fourth-grade daughter's concert, or your most important convention always took you out of town on your wedding anniversary. Maybe it's the outfit that you got at a sale but it still cost "too much." You think you have forgotten such events, but they come back weeks or months into the newly minted marriage, and you start picking up the old rocks and hurling them at each other.

How do you overcome this tendency? You have to agree that since you have been reconciled and are remarried, the past is forgotten. You will not use the past to hurt each other. When you find yourself tempted to do this, remove yourself geographically from your spouse's presence if that is what it takes. When you are cooled off, ask forgiveness and recommit to keeping the past out. Those are decisions you can make, and they will make a major difference in the temperature of your marriage.

3. Watching for Old Differences

I find that remarried couples can still fight about a lot of the old differences they used to have. Both the husband and wife are keenly aware of the trigger points at which those differences become fights.

Remarrieds can get really discouraged about this. When they find themselves replaying an old fight, they suddenly think, *Oh, we're back where we were before. This marriage is going to come apart again*. No, that is not necessary. You need to employ the new relational skills you have learned during the period before the marriage. You deal with the old problems, but you come up with different conclusions from the ones you reached under the old regime. If you have become Christians during the process of reconciliation, you also have the Holy Spirit to help you.

4. No Beauty Contest, Please

Judy has had a weight problem for many years, and it has contributed to her poor self-image. After the reconciliation, she made deliberate efforts to lose weight, usually unsuccessfully. The security provided by a committed husband eventually helped her achieve a measure of success.

The fact is that a lot of men are concerned as they see their wives getting heavier or grayer with age. They want their wives to look physically beautiful forever. Yet these same men never see themselves as getting older, losing their hair or their teeth, having a hearing loss, or developing protruding stomachs.

The husband really needs to help his wife work her way through a weight problem. If she has to go on a diet, he needs to be willing to restrict his food intake. If she needs physical exercise, he should volunteer to walk with her. He should also look in the mirror to see how attractive he's keeping himself for his wife!

5. Children

After you remarry, your children may well have a tendency to add to the stress of the renewed relationship. After all, their values and freedom have been affected by your getting together again. They can no longer play one against the other to obtain special favors. In fact, you can now gang up on them—at least that's what it may seem like to them.

You can expect that when you reconcile and remarry, your children will have a real struggle. Girls especially may have had Mom to themselves so much that Dad becomes an unwelcome interloper. Yet that period will last only so long. Children will adapt to a changed environment if you both stay firm. They will accept the reality of the new atmosphere in the home, just as they eventually accepted your remarriage.

Now mind you, I did not say they would *like* the new atmosphere, just as they may not have liked your remarrying. So you may find them accepting the situation without any enthusiasm while recognizing the reality in it.

Jim and Bonnie's remarriage provides a typical illustration of new stresses for the children. Bonnie is a school teacher. When she gets home in the evening, the last thing she wants to do is pester the girls about cleaning up their room. So for the nearly six years of the divorce, they basically maintained their own level of neatness.

Then Jim—the neatnik—showed up again. When he comes home, he cannot stand to see his daughters' things scattered around. The resulting interaction with the girls was downright unpleasant at first. Yet they have come to realize that Dad is home to stay and his attitude toward neatness is important.

Be sure that you set the ground rules for authority in the home before the remarriage. Determine that you will support each other, even when your spouse has made what you consider to be an unwise decision in relationship to the children (unless it brings them into physical or spiritual danger). You may well want to discuss the decision when the children are in bed and decide on a change. Then it will be Mom's *and* Dad's decision.

6. Different Spiritual Speeds

Most of you were not in tune with each other spiritually before the divorce. Developing a spiritually alive and mature relationship requires a strong commitment to each other's spiritual growth. And that is rare.

Typically, the wife in a divorce situation stays with her church, or she sows her wild oats and then returns to the church. Not so the husband, who is usually very slow to come back, often because he tends to feel responsible that the divorce happened. Because of this, you should agree to operate spiritually on the level of the slower developing person.

Recognizing this, we have a policy at our church that may seem unnecessarily restrictive to the wife. We will not permit the wife to be part of an evening home Bible study without her husband. If we provide her growth opportunities for which her husband is not ready, the marriage will soon grow apart. We can put so much stress on the relationship that they are back to square one.

We do encourage women to get involved in women's daytime Bible study fellowship and women's meetings. We urge them to read their Bibles at home, but not to be out of the home on weeknights. If you have an unsaved husband and he does not want you to attend church, nourish your soul in the privacy of your home.

Some people recommend that the wife of an unsaved man should come to church, even though her husband is opposed. And even if her husband does not want her to tithe, she should tithe. As pastoral staff, we are convinced that with that kind of advice we are tearing marriages apart, instead of capitalizing on the evangelistic opportunity an unsaved spouse represents. When a committed, faithful wife honors her husband, she creates an aroma of holiness in her home.

The Joy in Remarriage

Remarriage can bring a lot of joy to both husband and wife. With the animosity gone and the sharp differences reduced, the partnership in marriage will bring out the best in both.

John and Judy are both active in the church and in classes for divorced people. They worship together, alone, and with other church members. They reach out in love and caring to many who have gone through divorce.

"Some of the insights John has gained into helping other people are marvelous. He also puts them into practice. It makes me really proud to see him doing that, for I know he would never have done that seven years ago," says Judy.

At the same time John is aware of significant growth in his wife.

"I have seen change in some big areas. It has been a joy to see her self-image improving greatly, helping her see who she is in the light of who God says she is," says John.

Such joy in seeing the marriage partner grow and develop is one of the most exciting aspects of remarriage. I do not see it with every couple who remarry because some couples are slow to mature in their new relationship, but the majority of those who are divorced and remarry a former spouse are making exciting progress. Their lives are enriched beyond anything they dreamed possible in the years before the divorce or during the period of separation and divorce.

When divorced persons marry again without seriously considering the possibility of reconciliation and remarriage, they may well be shortchanging themselves. Yes, I keep hearing about the glorious new relationships divorced singles are entering into—and the marvelous freedom they have with a new spouse. Based on what I know, I have to wonder if reconciliation and remarriage with the former spouse could not have produced the same results, or even superior ones. John and Judy, Jim and Bonnie, certainly would testify to that.

God is in the business of reconciling people to Himself and to one another. I like to believe He knows what He is about when He challenges us to be reconciled to one another. The writer to the Hebrews gives the reason for my optimism:

For we do not have a high priest who cannot sympathize with our weaknesses, but one who has been tempted in all things as we are, yet without sin. Let us therefore draw near with confidence to the throne of grace, that we may receive mercy and may find grace to help in time of need (Heb. 4:15-16).

Begin to think about your differences in new terms. Think of them as *reconcilable* instead of *irreconcilable*, a favored legal term these days. You can be reconciled when you have the reconciling Christ living in you through the Holy Spirit, and you can achieve a harmony in your relationship that may have been missing for a long time. That is my goal for you and that is what God intends for you. I urge you to take the first steps toward reconciliation today.

171

Reconciliation Discussion

BEFORE YOU BEGIN

This program is focused on struggling marriages, separated, or finally divorced couples. Some of the couples who have gone through this material have been able to move from a point of hatred and bitterness to at least being civil to each other in public. Others have maintained their friendship even though they have decided not to start a dating relationship. A few divorced couples have used the material in the full workbook version, *Reconciliation Instruction*, under the direction of an instructor to help them reconcile their differences and eventually remarry. Whatever your circumstance, this material may help you learn how to establish a healthy, enduring friendship or relationship with the person to whom you are or have been married.

THE DEFINITION OF RECONCILIATION IS NOT REMARRIAGE, BUT TO CAUSE TO BE FRIENDLY AND TO BRING BACK HARMONY

What is Reconciliation Discussion?

Reconciliation discussion is not premarital counseling for remarriage! Rather, it is designed to help you learn how to reconcile the past **before** you seriously consider another commitment to your ex or anyone else. By helping you better know yourself and your partner, Reconciliation Discussion enables you to think objectively about how to stabilize a marriage or deal responsibly with the separation or final divorce.

How Can I Use This Guide?

The eight sessions of "reconciliation discussion" are scheduled for every other week, giving you one full week to do the homework and the following week for you and your partner to meet for a time of discussion. The effectiveness of this material will depend upon the time you put into the homework and how thoroughly you discuss it when you meet together. Honesty is vital to the quality and longevity of any relationship. Meeting every other week gives you ample time to read and think about the topics that are assigned. If you move at a faster pace, you eliminate the opportunity for the material to penetrate the relationship and produce positive results. The four-month time period is vital to the process of evaluation, application, growth, and emotional adjustment.

Most emotionally devastating divorces and broken relationships can be prevented if both people will give themselves time to become friends. If this material is used properly, you will find that even if your relationship or marriage ends, you can remain good friends. This is helpful not only to you and your partner, but also to your mutual friends and families. A relationship or marriage that ends explosively affects everyone.

Let me emphasize that Reconciliation Discussion as presented in this material is not intended to take the place of marriage counseling. It can, however, provide a stable basis of evaluation upon which a couple can decide if they want to discuss the concept of spending the rest of their lives together. When the material is completed you will decide if you want to continue the friendship, pursue the relationship, or go your separate ways. If your divorce is final, remarriage may be appropriate. You can both benefit greatly from going through both the complete four-month workbook *Reconciliation Instruction* program and premarital counseling, should your relationship lead toward remarriage. If used correctly, reconciliation discussion can lead to a vital and growing relationship at best, or to a warm, long-lasting friendship at the very least. Remember, the bond between formally married people is only broken by death.

How Do I Get Started?

The initial steps are very easy. You both must read the following prerequisites, sign the written commitment form, and set up your first appointment. Then meet every other week and follow the discussion agenda for each of the eight sessions.

INTRODUCTORY SESSION
Prerequisites

1. You and your partner must have a strong desire to work toward a peaceful resolution of your relationship.
2. You must be willing to meet for an introductory meeting and eight sessions, which will be scheduled every other week for approximately four months.
3. You must be willing to do one to two hours of homework one

week and spend one to two hours the following week discussing the homework.

4. No changes are to be made in the legal status of the relationship. If you are living separately, continue that for the next four months. Neither is to file, and if the papers have been filed you are to contact the attorney and put the process on hold.

5. If finally divorced do not discuss remarriage subjectively between the two of you, even while discussing marriage in Session Six. This may be difficult, but it is vital in order to protect the relationship from unrealistic expectations and undue pressure.

6. Be willing to become mutually exclusive, no relational one-on-one time with anyone else of the opposite sex. This means no luncheon dates, calls, gifts, one-on-one time, or notes to anyone other than the person going through this with you. If there is another relationship you must be willing to tell the other person about this four-month commitment and stop that relationship.

7. All subjects, assignments, and discussions are to be confidential to protect the integrity of the relationship.

8. Even if the relationship breaks down, your commitment to reconciliation discussion must continue for the eight sessions. This is to prevent either one of you from getting hurt, and to test your commitment level.

9. Agree to spend at least these *minimum* hours together each month:

First month:	10 hours	Third month:	30 hours
Second month:	20 hours	Fourth month:	40 hours

Time alone is counted hour for hour; group time is divided by four; phone time is counted when the conversation runs over half an hour. Time together is to be recorded by the man on the monthly time charts. The total should exceed the minimum of 140 hours in the next four months.

10. Be honest about the physical part of the relationship. Circle the number that represents the highest level of physical involvement you are willing to go to: Seven is the maximum you can choose unless you are legally married.

(1) Look
(2) Touch
(3) Lightly holding hands
(4) Constantly holding hands
(5) Light kiss

(6) Strong kiss
(7) French kiss
(8) Fondling breasts
(9) Fondling sexual organs
(10) Sexual intercourse

Each person is to list the highest level that they are willing to be physically involved. She (_____) He (_____) The physical relationship is controlled by the slower person, so the lowest number is the limit on the relationship during this four-month program. This number can only be changed if both parties agree to a new number and communicate this to each other.

11. If your divorce is final we ask that you make a commitment to keep the physical level at number 7 or below. This is to protect the relationship from being destroyed by excessive physical involvement.

12. If not currently married and the physical level exceeds number 7 you both must be willing to fill out the Moral Purity Worksheet in this section. If you have a pastor, the man must be willing to contact him within twenty-four hours after exceeding the physical limits. If the man does not do this, the woman should do so. Letting the pastor know is one way to protect the spiritual lives of both partners as well as the relationship.

Written Commitment

If you and your partner are both willing to accept the prerequisites and to commit yourselves to reconciliation discussion sign and date both workbooks.

Signed _____ Dated _____

Signed _____ Dated _____

In the course of this material if you are totally unable to go on, fill out this sheet and discuss it with your partner. This is the only way to exit this program. Be aware that this is a very serious breach of commitment.

Vows

1. Dictionary definition of a vow:
2. Write out the following verses in your own words.

a. Ecclesiastes 5:4–5
b. Numbers 30:2
c. Deuteronomy 23:21–23
3. List your reasons for wanting out of this commitment:

Guidelines for Monthly Time Charts

The purpose of the time chart is to provide you with a useful way to keep track of the amount of time you spend together each month. By putting some minimums on time spent together, you will appreciate being together and you will find that the relationship may have been starved to death by the business of your schedules.

The man should begin keeping the chart after you both sign the written commitment. The date of the next day should be entered in the first upper left hand space; below that, enter the day of the week. Continue throughout the month. Follow the example on the right side of the chart.

One-on-One Time

This includes times when you are alone together, whether in public or private. Even if other people are around, you are alone unless you are interacting with them. One-on-one times includes movies, dinners, picnics, and long rides.

Group Time

Consider times when the two of you are interacting with others, such as on double dates, at church, with your children, or when working in a group, as group time. The key word is *interacting*. Speaking to the couple at the next table during dinner is not interacting.

Phone Time

More than thirty minutes on the phone together is recorded as one-on-one time because of the impact that long, in-depth discussions have on a relationship.

The time charts are just one of many tools you will find in this material, but their effectiveness is determined by how completely and honestly they are maintained. They should be reviewed together on a regular basis, and you should both agree on how time together is counted. Also note the shaded section after 2:00 A.M. If you are divorced and need to be together after these hours, it is important that you be in a group setting or a public environment. This helps to avoid the appearance of evil (1 Thess. 5:22).

FIGURE 2-4
MONTHLY TIME CHART

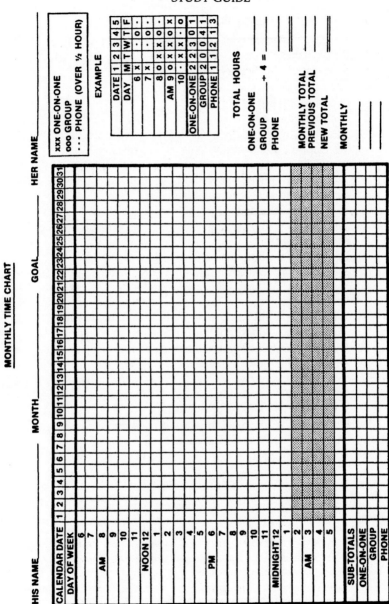

177

MORAL PURITY WORKSHEET

To be used if physical contact exceeds the biblical limits agreed to in the Prerequisites.

1. What are the dictionary definitions of:
   a. Purity
   b. Immorality
   c. Fornication
2. Read Ephesians 5:1-17. According to this passage, how should we respond to fornication?
3. Read 1 Thessalonians 4:1-7. What is God's will for us?
4. Read 1 Corinthians 5:1-8. What should the church do about sexual immorality among its members?
5. Read 1 Corinthians 6:13-20. What should we do?
6. Read James 5:16. Is it important for us to be honest with others about our sin?
7. Rephrase 1 Corinthians 10:13 in your own words.
8. List any ways of escape from temptation that God provided but that you did not use. Remember that God promises to provide escape.
9. What steps could be taken to help prevent recurrence?
10. Should you further limit your time alone together?
11. Have you confessed your failure to God and also asked forgiveness from the other person?
12. Evaluate the negative results this involvement has had on the relationship.
13. What places should be off-limits?
14. Does being married before make it right before God?
15. Are you involved in fornication?
16. What do you need to do?

SESSION ONE

Assignment: Read Chapters One and Two

Discussion Agenda

Note: Be aware that these first sessions may seem a little shallow but that each session will contribute to a deepening of the relationship as you progress.

1. Open the session with prayer for direction and mutual understanding. I suggest that the man take the lead here.

2. If either of you has not completed the homework, confirm this meeting when the work is completed.
3. Carefully discuss each other's definitions of love, and note your reactions to the answers.
4. Ask questions and check your conclusions as you review the autobiographies.
5. Discuss the questions for Chapter One and Two.
6. Be sure the monthly time chart is up to date and that you both agree on the data. Should you make any changes in time spent together?
7. Review the assignments for the next session, and clarify any areas of concern.
8. Close this session in prayer.

Word Study—Love

1. What is the dictionary definition of *love?*
2. Define these Greek words for *love* (ask a Christian friend or pastor if necessary).
   a. *Phileo* (love of friends):
   b. *Eros* (physical love):
   c. *Agape* (total love):
3. First Corinthians 13 describes love as:
4. Give an example of love from the Gospel of John:
5. Look up and explain two Scripture verses on love (a concordance may be helpful):

Autobiography

   a. Childhood
   b. Teenage years
   c. College age years
   d. Adult years
   e. Dream vacation
   f. Describe the kind of person you want to be in fifteen years.

Chapter One Questions

Discuss your definition and the book's definition of the following:
   a. Friendship
   b. Relationship
   c. Marriage

d. Divorce

e. Reconciliation

Chapter Two Questions

1. After reading the section "Heritage of Memories," what specific positive events came across your mind?
2. What negative emotions have you retained that you want to remove from the relationship between you and your partner?
3. Have your children or close family members encouraged or discouraged reconciliation between you and your partner?
4. How does reconciling with your partner make economic sense to you?
5. How can reconciliation with your partner contribute to the stability in your own life?
6. What do you think God expects of you in your relationship with your partner?

SESSION TWO

Assignment: Chapter Three

Discussion Agenda

1. Pray together for God's direction during this meeting and for each other in general.
2. Discuss how you view your friendship. You do not have to agree on everything. As Jim Weatherford says, "If you both agree on everything, one of you isn't necessary." The key is to understand each other's viewpoint, not necessarily to change it.
3. Review any differences in your answers to the questions on Chapter Three. Discuss them thoroughly.
4. Be honest as you share your feelings, and listen carefully to each other. This is a good time to check how well you are communicating by using the phrase, "Let me be sure I understand . . ." and then repeating what you thought the other person just said. Let them respond to your conclusions.
5. For those who are not legally married or have agreed to a lower number: Have you exceeded your number on the physical involvement list? If the answer is no, encourage one another and continue to monitor your time together. If yes, and you are not legally married please refer to the Moral Purity Worksheet. If you

are having trouble in this area, you seriously need to consider enlisting a friend or instructor who can hold you accountable. If the relationship is valuable to you, it should be brought under control. You may want to consider the supervised *Reconciliation Instruction* program.

6. Review the monthly time chart, and use it to evaluate where and when you spend your time together. Are you avoiding the appearance of evil (1 Thess. 5:22)? Look at things from your neighbor's perspective. Discuss the relationship between long periods of time alone together and increased physical involvement.

7. Share one positive thing you have learned about the other person in this session.

8. Are you spending enough time together? Too much?

9. Review your next assignments and close in prayer.

Friendship Evaluation

1. How did you meet?
2. How would you describe the level of your friendship?
   a. In the past?
   b. At the present?
3. What are the strengths and weaknesses of the friendship?

Chapter Three Questions

1. Discuss the three stages of marriage:
   a. The romantic stage
   b. The disenchantment stage
   c. The accommodation stage
2. Discuss the chart on progression of relationships:
   a. For men
   b. For women
3. In one sentence, summarize the principle of the Talley-Graph.
4. Give a personal example of the principle.
5. Explain *homeostasis*.
6. After reading Psalm 139:1-4, explain how you are not alone in your attempt to reconcile with your former spouse.
7. How would you rate yourself regarding the following issues: (Poor—Average—Good—Excellent)
   a. Self-image

b. Ability to function as an individual
c. Ability to deal with conflict
d. Spiritual relationship
e. Ability to resolve conflict

SESSION THREE

Assignment: Read Chapters Four and Five

Discussion Agenda

1. The woman should open with prayer, asking God to help both of you visualize the plan that He has for your lives.
2. Review each others' goals carefully. Does the direction of a person's life and of his dreams help you to know him?
3. Go over the commitment study very carefully.
4. Compare your answers for Chapter Four and Five of *Reconcilable Differences*. Have you been able to develop any of the conflict resolving skills that are needed for a quality relationship? Are you able to relate to each other on a spiritual level?
5. Go over the monthly time chart together. Be sure it is current and that you both agree on how the time is being recorded.
6. Pray and thank God for one special quality in your partner's life.

Goal Planning

A goal is a future event that can be accomplished in a given time, and by which our progress can be measured. We need goals to help us arrive at what God wants us to be. Our goals help us to accomplish what we set out to do. Your life goal should be measurable in a time frame as well. The time frame is your life span, generally about seventy years.

1. Do you have a life goal?
2. What is it?
3. What do you believe God wants you to be doing, or to have accomplished, in fifteen to twenty years?
4. In reaching toward your goal, describe what progress you want to make within five years?
5. What practical short-range goals should you plan to accomplish this year toward your life goal?
6. In the next six months?
7. In the next three months?
8. This month?

Commitment Study

1. Respond to the following statement: "I am committed to God's best for your life, even if that means I cannot be a part of it." Can you say this to your partner honestly? Why or why not?
2. Give three actions that indicate commitment:
   a. By him, toward her
   b. By her, toward him
3. Give three actions that indicate a lack of commitment:
   a. By him, toward her
   b. By her, toward him

Chapter Four Questions

1. Disharmony can result from unmet expectations in marriage. Do you feel having unrealistic expectations contributed to your disharmony? If so, give two areas in which you feel you got something you "didn't bargain for."
2. Now, share one area in which you might have "surprised" your partner by not meeting their expectations for marriage.
3. What is your definition of quality time spent with your spouse?

Chapter Five Questions

1. Are you on the line of reconciliation?
2. Have you ever cycled away from the line?
3. Are they on the line of reconciliation?
4. Have they ever cycled away from the line?
5. Itemize several meanings of love from 1 Corinthians 13.

SESSION FOUR

Assignment: Read Chapter Six

Discussion Agenda

1. The man should open this meeting in prayer that both of you will be open to the will of God.
2. Share with each other the five changes God wants to make in your lives. Compare individually what three things you feel God wants to change in your partners life. This is designed to improve your conflict resolving skills.
3. Discuss The Onset of Disharmony from Chapter Six of *Reconcilable Differences*. Can you now pinpoint with greater clarity the kinds of reactions that escalate disagreements? Can you list some

suggestions of how to avoid reaching the danger level of disharmony?

4. For those who are not legally married or have agreed to a lower number: Have you exceeded your number on the physical involvement list? If the answer is no, encourage each other, and continue to monitor your time together. If yes, change your number or refer to the Moral Purity Worksheet in the beginning section.

5. State how you think the other person is doing in regard to this situation in general and your relationship in particular. Discuss and evaluate any changes you feel God wants you to make.

6. Pray for each other about the changes that God wants to make in their life.

Self-Improvement

1. List five changes you feel God wants to make in your life:

2. List three changes you feel God wants to make in your partner's life:

Chapter Six Questions

1. Rate your self control in the following areas:
   (Poor—Average—Good—Excellent)
   a. Sexual
   b. Romantic
   c. Financial
   d. Physical
   e. Spiritual

2. Becoming stable again requires building a new life as a mature single adult. Are you content as a single person (divorced or separated)?

3. How have you improved yourself as a single?

4. How have you seen your partner improve as a single?

SESSION FIVE

Assignment: Read Chapter Seven

Discussion Agenda

1. Opening prayer by the woman will help get the session moving.
2. Discuss any conflicts that may have arisen so far. Are you able to understand each other's viewpoints and resolve differences?
3. Review the answers about finances even if it seems a little redundant. Be aware that disagreements in this area are a major cause of divorce.
4. Compare your differences on the spiritual evaluation sheet. In what areas do you need to grow? How can you help each other?
5. Review the questions for Chapter Seven.
6. By now the material should be drawing the two of you into deeper involvement. This will increase the tension in some areas of the relationship, but learning to handle the tension is important in the development of a strong and enduring relationship.
7. Discuss your reasons for keeping your relationship at the line of reconciliation.
8. Pray for each other's spiritual life and the ability to love each other as an act of the will.

Finances

1. Was your checkbook balanced to the penny last month? Has it ever been?
2. Give your approximate net worth in thousands:
   15——25——50——75——100——150+
3. Do you owe more than you are worth?
4. Have you refinanced your house or bills in the last five years?
5. Have you ever been in bankruptcy?   Year _____ Amount _____
6. Do you have a savings account balance over $500?
7. Do you have a retirement fund?
8. Are you in debt to any relatives? Amount _____
9. Do you tithe on your net or gross income?
10. Do you pay alimony or child support? Amount _____
    Current? yes _____ no _____
11. Have you ever had property foreclosed on? Date?

12. Do any of your loans or transactions have large balloon payments in the future?
13. Do you have a will? Where would your estate go if you died today?
14. Have you changed the beneficiaries of your estate?
15. Do you expect your mate to combine financial resources with you?
16. Discuss all debts with balances over $100.

Spiritual Evaluation Form

1. Summarize your family's spiritual heritage.
2. How did you become a Christian?
3. Highlight your spiritual growth pattern for the last five years.
4. Evaluate the following:
   (Poor—Average—Good—Excellent)
   a. Quiet Time
   b. Prayer
   c. Scripture memory
   d. Witnessing
   e. Control of bad habits
   f. Stewardship (tithe)
   g. Church attendance
   h. Spiritual leadership roles
   i. Bible study
5. To whom are you spiritually accountable?
6. What is one of your spiritual gifts?

Chapter Seven Questions

1. Evaluate the different cycles that men and women go through in a relationship.
2. Review some of the specific differences between men's and women's cycles.
3. What is the key word for men? For women?

SESSION SIX

Assignment: Read Chapters Eight and Nine

Discussion Agenda

1. Opening prayer by the man will help get the session moving.

2. Discuss any hindrances that you each may have about moving toward friendship.
3. Review the worksheet on marriage.
4. Discuss the questions on Chapters Eight and Nine.
5. Pray for each other's spiritual life and the ability to be friendly toward one another.

Hindrances

1. Give five of your own personal hindrances for not moving closer together or remarrying.
2. Give three of the other person's hindrances.

Word Study—Marriage

1. How many times have you been married?
2. When did you become a growing Christian?
3. Was your last spouse a growing Christian?
4. When did your last spouse become a growing Christian?
5. Who filed for your last divorce? Where?
6. Was there fornication (adultery, homosexuality, or incest) on your part before the divorce was final?
7. Was your spouse involved in fornication?
8. Read aloud and discuss the following verses: Matthew 19:9, Matthew 5:32, 1 Corinthians 7:10–11, Deuteronomy 24:4.
9. Are you scripturally free to remarry another mate? On what grounds?
10. Is the other person in this relationship scripturally free to marry another mate? On what grounds?
11. If you had followed your parents' advice, would you have gotten married the last time?
12. What steps have you made toward reconciliation?

Chapter Eight Questions

1. During a period of emotional upheaval, you need to take the time to develop a plan of action. Review the steps you think you need to take to help your life move forward positively.
2. In what areas can you be a giver instead of a taker?
3. Do you feel that God is capable of helping you change for the sake of the relationship? How?
4. Are you free to date?

Chapter Nine Questions

1. At what level of friendship were you and your partner when you were first married?
2. At what level of friendship are you now with your partner?
3. In your opinion, what does "friendship is a balance" really mean?
4. Review the five hindrances to developing friendships.
5. Quiz each other on five of the eight "friendship enhancers."

SESSION SEVEN

Assignment: Read Chapter Ten

Discussion Agenda

1. The woman should open in prayer for God's wisdom.
2. Review the topic of children. Be honest—this is one of the major causes of divorce!
3. Share your prayers with each other. Review how each of you views the relationship up to this point. Is the relationship improving and deepening or becoming shallow?
4. Evaluate the monthly time chart. Do you need to make any changes in when, where, or how much time you are spending together?
5. Review the assignments for the next session, and discuss what you plan to write in your summary letter.
6. Pray for one another.

Children

1. Do you like children?
2. Do you want more children?
3. If you both had custody of all your children under the age of eighteen, how many children would you have?
4. Do you believe in corporal punishment (spanking)?
5. How much influence should a child have on a parent's decision to reconcile or remarry?

Moral Purity

1. Read the following passages, and comment on what God says about moral purity:

   1 Corinthians 5:9-13 Hebrews 12:15-17
   2 Corinthians 12:19-21 James 1:14-15

188

Ephesians 4:22–24   1 John 2:16
1 Thessalonians 4:1–7

2. What does God say about sexual temptation in the following verses: 1 Corinthians 6:18–20, 1 Corinthians 10:13, 1 Peter 2:11–12.
3. Why do people often rush into a relationship?
4. Define the following types of relationships:
Natural   Sensual   Lustful
5. Evaluate two problems in allowing a relationship or marriage to break up.
6. What do you think causes a relationship to break up?
7. When in your marriage did you notice a struggle with "who has the authority?"
8. Thinking back over your marriage, can you now see some of the causes of your misconceptions?
9. What are you willing to give up now that you were not willing to give up before?

Chapter Ten Questions

1. Why is it so hard to keep on doing right?
2. How do you protect yourself when others back away?
3. Why is rejection such an important part of this process?
4. What does *forgive* really mean?

SESSION EIGHT

Assignment: Read Chapter Eleven and Twelve

Discussion Agenda

Your commitment not to talk or think about moving back together or remarrying each other is now completed. You should be able to openly discuss your options and select a new direction.

1. The man should open this meeting in prayer that both you and your partner will be open to the will of God.
2. Discuss Chapters Eleven and Twelve in *Reconcilable Differences* and share your answers with each other. Be sure to listen to the other person's answers.
3. Share how you feel you could improve your friendship.
4. Review the new direction.
5. Discuss the evaluation.
6. Read each other's summary page.

7. Share prayer concerns in the area of becoming more friendly and pray for each other's needs.

Chapter Eleven Questions

1. Why should you consider reconciliation?
2. What are the four stages?
3. Are you willing to sign a four-month commitment to go through the complete *Reconciliation Workbook* program?
4. Is your partner willing to sign a four-month commitment to go through the complete *Reconciliation Workbook* program?

Chapter Twelve Questions

1. If you are not moving together what do you plan to do?
2. Who is the most committed at this point?
3. Are you going too fast? Is your partner?
4. If you are not legally married, has there been sexual intercourse?
5. What is the most effective plan for the children?
6. How long should you wait at the line of reconciliation?

New Direction

You need to give your honest responses to each of the options below for your future direction together.

1. Friendship:
   Pro   Con
2. Relationship:
   Pro   Con
3. Consider taking the complete four month *Reconciliation Instruction* Course:
   Pro   Con
4. Consider moving together or remarrying your partner:
   Pro   Con
5. His direction is:
6. Her direction is:
7. Together we have agreed to:

Evaluation

1. What was the most beneficial part of "Reconciliation Discussion" for you?
2. What material or session was the least helpful?

3. What changes would you make in your relationship if you could do it over?
4. Give two examples of how this instruction has affected your life.
5. Would you recommend this material to others?
6. For those who are not legally married, did you exceed number 7? If yes, were you able to bring the level of physical involvement back down?
7. What direction for the relationship did you choose?
8. Write a one-page summary of how this instruction has affected your life and mail it to Rev. Jim A. Talley, Ph.D.

Congratulations, you have survived the course!

About the Author

Dr. Jim A. Talley was formerly the associate minister of single adults at First Baptist Church in Modesto, California. He is currently in private practice in Oklahoma City, Oklahoma, and teaches seminars on the dynamics of interpersonal relationships. He and his wife, Joyce, were married in 1961. They have three children and six grandchildren.

Talley is the author of five books including *Too Close Too Soon* with Bobbie Reed (Thomas Nelson, 1989), which has sold more than 100,000 copies. Study material based on Talley's books is available for mature lay leaders who wish to teach sound relationship principles for dating couples (*Too Close Too Soon*) or estranged couples (*Reconcilable Differences*). For more information, write to the author at:

> **Relationship Resources, Inc.**
> 11805 Sylvester Drive
> Oklahoma City, OK 73162-1018
> Phone: (405) 720-8300
> Fax: (405) 728-1666
> E-mail: drtalley@drtalley.com

The author can also be contacted at the Internet website for Relationship Resources, Inc., at:

> http://www.drtalley.com